DURKHEIM AND WOMEN

DURKHEIM

AND WOMEN

Jennifer M. Lehmann

▪ University of Nebraska Press
Lincoln and London

The paper in this book meets the minimum requirements
of American National Standard for Information Sciences—
Permanence of Paper for Printed Library Materials,
ANSI Z39.48-1984.

Library of Congress Cataloging-in-Publication Data
Lehmann, Jennifer M., 1956–
    Durkheim and women / Jennifer M. Lehmann.
        p.   cm.
    Includes bibliographical references and index.
    ISBN 0-8032-2907-0
    1. Durkheim, Emile, 1858–1917—Views on women.
    2. Women—Social conditions.   3. Sociology—History.
        I. Title.
HQ1154.L427   1994   305.42—dc20   93-29360
                                                 CIP

To my mother,
  Mildred N. Lehmann,
  who is one of my enduring
  role models

CONTENTS

ACKNOWLEDGMENTS

I must begin by expressing my profound gratitude to the people who reviewed this manuscript. Roslyn W. Bologh, Ruth A. Wallace, and Rosalind A. Sydie are scholars whose evaluations of this work are tremendously important to me. Each of them provided extremely thorough, thoughtful, and helpful comments, questions, and suggestions in the most constructive and supportive manner imaginable. A fourth, anonymous, reviewer provided the toughest criticisms and challenges and deserves the most credit for the positive features of the completed manuscript. Specifically, this reviewer insisted that I research Durkheim's historical context, and this research culminated in chapter 1. I believe this chapter radically changes and improves the book, and I would not have written it had I not been "forced."

In addition to the reviewers, the copyeditor, Alice Bennett, made substantial improvements in the final version of the manuscript. Her expertise in matters of grammar and punctuation compensated for my ignorance in these matters, and her painstaking and rigorous labors compensated for my own inattention to detail.

I would also like to recognize the sustained support I receive from my academic colleagues. Ben Agger at suny/Buffalo continues to serve as my academic support system, and he deserves the most credit for the positive features of my academic career. Cindy Lamberts-Anderson, Lynn White, Helen Moore, Laura Sanchez, Mary Jo Deegan, Suzanne Ortega, Moira Ferguson, Beth Anne Shelton, Sonia Partridge, Shahrzad Bazargan, Karen Kelly, Patrice Engelbrecht, Kathy Branchaud, and the Women's Studies Faculty at the University of Nebraska continue to infuse me with knowledge, insight, inspiration, and good humor. As both colleagues and friends, they provide me with cherished role models and precious companionship.

I shall pause here and acknowledge the contributions of some of the women "behind every great man." For Durkheim, they include Mélanie Isidor Durkheim, Durkheim's "absent" mother; Louise Dreyfus Durkheim, his "absent" wife and collaborator; and Marie Durkheim, his "absent" daughter.

Finally, I acknowledge my own family: Wesley A. Lehmann, Mildred N. Lehmann, and Jonathan W. Lehmann. It is ultimately for them that I do what I do, and it is ultimately because of them that I am able to do what I do.

DURKHEIM AND WOMEN

Chapter 1

DURKHEIM'S

MILIEU

▪ I will begin my twentieth-century fin-de-siècle examination of Durkheim's nineteenth-century fin-de-siècle theories of women by looking back two centuries, to the eighteenth-century fin-de-siècle events of the French Revolution.[1] In particular, I want to explore the relationship between the French Revolution and its aftermath, and women. The "official" French Revolution occurred in 1789 and is commemorated on July 14, the date the Bastille prison was overrun in Paris. The participation of women in the French Revolution was at this point substantial and significant. During the "October Days" of 1789, for example, "thousands of market women, housewives, and working women . . . marched to Versailles in search of bread. . . . 'Let them eat cake' was Marie Antoinette's famous reply" (Boxer and Quataert 1987, 109).

Joan B. Landes describes the October Days as the occasion when "a large crowd of Parisian market women and national guardsmen march from Paris to Versailles and bring the royal family back to the capital" (1988, 93). She goes on to describe the tremendous importance of this "momentous" march: "At the very least, the women's action strengthened the constitutional forces within the nation and prepared the groundwork for the republican movement" (109–10).

The initial alliance between women and French republicanism extended beyond women's participation in revolutionary insurrections, and beyond the borders of France. In 1790, in England, Mary Wollstonecraft published *A Vindication of the Rights of Man*. This work was a liberal defense of the French Revolution, in response to conservatives in general and Edmund Burke's conservative condemnation, *Reflections on the Revolution in France*, in particular. This work also signals the end of the honeymoon in the uneasy marriage of feminism and republicanism.

In September 1791 the first French Republican Constitution was formulated. Its preamble is the celebrated "Declaration of the Rights of Man and Citizen." The term "Man," like the term "Fraternity" in the revolutionary motto "Liberty, Equality, Fraternity," augurs ill for the fate of women, as the term "Citizen" augurs ill for women, workers, and other subordinate groups in Republican France. In fact, according to Landes, the constitution, a founding document of modernity and "democracy," "divided the populace between active and passive citizens on the basis of wealth, thereby excluding the large majority of male citizens from full political participation. . . . only males possessing the appropriate measure of property were eligible to exercise formal political liberties in the new nation. All women were assigned to the category of passive citizens" (Landes 1988, 122).

Later in 1791, Olympe de Gouges answered the "Declaration of the Rights of Man and Citizen" with her own declaration, "The Declaration of the Rights of Woman." Ironically, she addressed her declaration to Marie Antoinette, who was still queen of France. Neither the queen nor the republican revolutionaries paid heed to de Gouges's literary protest, however. "With the establishment in 1792 of the first French Republic, all males were granted universal suffrage, making even more pronounced the formal political exclusion of women which appeared in the constitution of 1791" (139). In 1792 Mary Wollstonecraft responded to the republican constitution, and the extension of suffrage to men only, with a second manifesto. Her *A Vindication of the Rights of Woman* is a founding statement of modern, liberal feminism, composed against rather than by the founding fathers of bourgeois democracy. Conversely, according to Landes, the French Republic was "constructed against women, not just without them" (171).

In February 1793 women in France, still determined to participate in republicanism and revolution alike, formed the Society of Revolutionary Republican Women (Landes 1988, 93). However, the remainder of 1793 was to prove fatal, to individual women and feminists, and to the star-crossed union of feminism and republicanism. On October 16 Marie Antoinette was executed. On October 30 the revolutionary government issued a decree abolishing all women's clubs and associations, rendering any political organization or activity on the part of women illegal. On November 3 Olympe de Gouges was executed, following Marie Antoinette to the guillotine. In another tragic irony, de Gouges had written in her "Declaration of the Rights of Women": "Woman has the right to mount the scaffold; she must equally have the right to mount the rostrum" (cited in Landes 1988, 126). In republican France the scaffold continued to level women and men in democratic equality, while the rostrum remained accessible exclusively to men.[2]

Approximately one hundred years elapsed between the commencement of the French Revolution in 1789 and the commencement of Durkheim's sociological writing in 1885.[3] Nineteenth-century France was characterized by intense social turmoil and constant, dramatic social change. Karen Offen characterizes this epoch in French history in the following way: "French political history during the nineteenth century was marked by continual battles for control of the government. No regime founded in the wake of the French Revolution seemed able to survive more than 20 years. With the establishment of the Third Republic in the 1870's, the battles did not stop" (1987, 179–80). According to Landes, postrevolutionary French state structure "vacillated between dictatorship, constitutional monarchy, and republicanism, interspersed by moments of revolutionary upheaval and defeat" (1988, 171).

Two developments in the tumult of nineteenth-century France critically affected the condition of women. The first, in 1804, was the enactment of the Napoleonic Civil Code, which dramatically embodied that paradox of modernity, the marriage of liberalism and chauvinism: "The subordination of women to men and a rigid sexual differentiation were encapsulated in the uniform body of laws codified by Napoleon during the first decade of the century. The Civil Code excluded women from the definition of citizenship even as it recognized the equal rights of all citizens" (Landes 1988, 170).

The second development was the Revolution of 1830, which precipitated a resurgence of feminist mobilization. In France and elsewhere, feminism, along with diverse other social movements, thrived throughout the rest of the nineteenth century and into the twentieth, until the conservative nationalism of World War I definitively staved off progressive tendencies. Feminism, along with other social movements, flourished as a result of the past betrayals, and the promising future, of continual social fluctuation. As Landes writes, "Beginning in the 1830's, women organized collectively to demand redress from patriarchal institutions. . . . it was then that feminism acquired its modern shape and consciousness—as a reply to the refusal of both liberals and republicans to resolve the problem of women's civil and political subordination" (1988, 169).

There is a striking contrast between these contemporary feminist reconstructions of Durkheim's sociohistorical matrix and Durkheim's own constructions of his society. In a sense this is a contrast between the depiction of a very noisy—turbulent, conflictual, contested, oppressive, and revolutionary—society and the depiction of a very quiet—serene, cooperative, consensual, functional, and evolutionary—society. For Durkheim, social history is a silent process of evolution in which the social organism noiselessly differentiates into specialized organs and cells. Social structure is the silent morphological instrument of a silent physiological process in which these specialized organs and cells soundlessly perform mutually necessary and beneficial functions.

In fact one of the most distinctive features of Durkheim's narrative about social history and social structure is its profound silence. This silence perhaps reflects the silence of Durkheim's own "quiet, familial existence" in his bourgeois, patriarchal domicile where he observed silence except at meals (Lukes 1985, 99); where his work was the silent process of reading and writing; where he sat isolated, sheltered, and removed from the sounds of domestic labor, manual labor, and political confrontation.[4]

In any event, Durkheim is strangely and ominously silent about the severe political, economic, and ideological strife in France—about the fierce and violent struggles, revolts, and reactions that constituted a perpetual state of conflict between various hierarchical social orders and women, workers, racial minorities, and colonized peoples. Durkheim's narrative suppresses the noise of protest, of demonstration, of revolution and counterrevolution, of repression and resistance, of riots and rebellions, of imperialistic war and civil war, of legislative assemblies filled with vehement debates, of city streets filled with angry citizens (and noncitizens), of impassioned political speeches and spontaneous mass outcries. His written words stifle the sounds of domestic violence, of the factory and the sweatshop, of manning the barricades and storming the Bastille, of gunshots and guillotines, of prison chains and prison doors. These sounds marked the lives of women, workers, and ethnic minorities in France and the lives of enslaved or colonized indigenous peoples in the French empire.

The sounds in Durkheim's social theory are the sounds of silence, and the silence is particularly deafening with respect to women. In Durkheim's account of society women are largely absent, and when they do appear, however briefly and sporadically, they are consigned to the exterior of society, to the nonsocial sphere of biological reproduction. It is hard to imagine, on reading Durkheim, that women were active participants in all the French revolutions as well as in the crusade for feminism; that they were active participants in the French waged-labor force;[5] that French women wrote and spoke in the public sphere; and that they were rewarded and punished for their social participation as were French men. Women in nineteenth-century France were hired and fired, paid wages and exploited; they were imprisoned, beaten, shot in the streets, and executed. They gained and lost rights as a result of their political, economic, and ideological activities, as did their male counterparts.

5 ■

The Structural Context

To portray the contemporary milieu, as opposed to the historical antecedents,[6] of Durkheim's theory of society and his theory of women, I will begin with social structures and practices—the "material" context of Durkheim's work.[7] The French Revolution, all one hundred years of it, represents the classic, archetypal example of bourgeois, liberal, capitalist revolution against aristocracy, conservatism, and feudalism. It popularized itself and generalized its constituency by promoting itself as a revolution for universal human rights and proclaiming itself the agency of liberty, equality, and fraternity, for all individuals.

However, these claims and promises were ultimately broken, and the legacy of the French Revolution as of all bourgeois revolutions has been interminable struggle over definitions of liberty, equality, and fraternity definitions of "men," "citizens," "individuals," and "humans." The French Revolution in particular, and bourgeois revolutions in general, were merely the initial battles in a protracted and ongoing war over exclusion and inclusion—over the exclusion from or the extension of: rights, liberty, and equality, variously defined, vis-à-vis qualified and unqualified human beings, variously defined.

Capitalism has promised a utopia of universal individual liberty and equality. It has delivered only "equal opportunity," and that only to select individuals. Capitalism as an economic system, along with capitalist political, cultural, and familial structures, has excluded the working class, women, and internal and external subordinate, colonized cultures from its utopian covenant. This covenant has been salient primarily for individuals of the capitalist class, the male sex, dominant ethnic groups, and imperialist countries. Therefore, since its revolutionary inception, capitalism has been embattled, challenged from the right by feudalism, from the left by socialism, and generally, from below, by those groups it has excluded from political, economic, and cultural benefits.[8]

At the turn of the century, when Durkheim lived and wrote, capitalism was inextricably linked with patriarchy, racism, and imperialism. The pronounced existence of patriarchy is attested by Durkheim's writing itself, as well as by the writing of his contemporaries, which will be explored below. The existence of racism is illustrated by the notorious Dreyfus Affair, in which Durkheim was prominently involved, and which crystallized and dramatized deep racial, cultural, and political schisms and inequalities within an allegedly unified and egalitarian "French" "society." As for French imperialism, Boxer and Quataert provide the following appraisal:

> In the last third of the nineteenth century, the Europeans gobbled up Africa, much of Asia, and many islands of the Pacific at a dizzying rate. Britain alone acquired 4.7 million square miles of territory between 1870 and 1900; France amassed 3.5 million and the new German Empire one million. By the turn of the century, nearly one-half billion non-Western people were under the control of Western colonial administrations, although not without protracted and often bloody resistance by native populations. For many ordinary Europeans, and certainly in the eyes of the ruling classes, such successes pointed to unmistakable moral superiority. (1987, 187)

As this passage indicates, imperialism has always coexisted peacefully, with liberal capitalism, but also violently, with nationalist and internationalist resistance to imperialism. The same is true of all the interconnected systems of inequality that coalesced and were concealed under the rubrics of modernity, liberalism, individualism, democracy, freedom, and rationality—that is, under the auspices of "advanced," "higher," "civilized," "superior" societies. The class inequality of capitalism has always met resistance in the form of socialism; the sex inequality of patriarchy has always met resistance in the form of feminism; and the cultural/racial inequality of racism has always met resistance in the form of cultural/racial pluralism.

The French Third Republic, then, cannot be conceived of as monolithic; it contained a multiplicity of systems of inequality, each producing a multiplicity of responses among a multiplicity of social groups. To begin with, the capitalist industrial economy, the democratic republican polity, and the attendant liberal humanist ideology provoked the opposition of the newly dispossessed. Feudal landowners, agricultural workers, the aristocratic nobility, and the traditional Catholic clergy rallied around romanticism, reaction, counterrevolution, and the restoration of feudalism; around monarchy, aristocracy, and/or empire; and around Catholic theocracy.

At the other end of the political spectrum, some of the newly disenfranchised and disinherited opposed the matrix of capitalism, patriarchy, and colonialism, in part or in its entirety, in moderation or in the extreme. The working class, women, and racial/cultural/national colonies that took exception to social inequity had two broad avenues of response. In the first place, they could advocate reform, which generally entails extension of political, economic, and/ or cultural rights, freedom, and equality to more, or all, social groups—the inclusion of more or all social groups in "society."

7 ▪

Reform of liberal capitalism could take one of two forms. It could manifest itself as classic liberalism, or the support of individualistic, laissez-faire, competitive, decentralized pure or early capitalism ("free enterprise" capitalism), coupled with an insistence on consistency. That is, de jure equal opportunity and individual mobility in the public sector are sufficient, but they must be free of distortion or obstruction for all groups and individuals. Reform of liberal capitalism could also manifest itself as neoliberalism, or support for a statist, social, collective, centralized capitalism (late, state, or welfare capitalism), with a focus on de facto equal opportunity and the amelioration of extralegal factors impinging on equal opportunity.[9]

Alternatively, radical opposition to the Third Republic would obviously and necessarily involve extensive transformation of some or all of the structures in the constellation of capitalism, patriarchy, racialism, and colonialism. The most viable radical forces of opposition in Durkheim's era included socialists, feminists, and socialist feminists in France, as well as antislavery and anti-imperialist movements of indigenous people in French colonies.

The Discursive Context

I shall now examine the discourse on "the woman question" that constituted the discursive, ideological, theoretical, or "ideational" context of Durkheim's work.[10] To reconstruct this context I have drawn principally upon the primary sources provided in Susan Groag Bell and Karen M. Offen's two-volume collection *Women, the Family, and Freedom: The Debate in Documents* (1983).[11] In these documents I have found a great range of responses to capitalism, patriarchy, racialism, and colonialism and an even greater array of combinations and permutations of responses to this complex configuration of structures and to the real or ideal structural positions of women, workers, ethnic minorities, and colonials.

In all this complexity I distinguish a simple, general dichotomy between two basic and contrasting theoretical/political positions: antifeminism, or patriarchalism, and feminism, or antipatriarchalism. I identify Durkheim's theory of women as antifeminist and Durkheim as a proponent of patriarchy—an evaluation I hope to substantiate in subsequent chapters. I then compare his theoretical framework first with various forms of antifeminism and then with various forms of feminism, to situate him within the theoretical problematics specific to his historical conjuncture.[12]

- 8

I have described Durkheim's theory of women as antifeminist or patriarchal. Antifeminism or patriarchalism is related to a broader type of social theory, which I call conservatism. "Conservative" social theory dates to the capitalist challenge to feudalism, when conservatives were those who wished to conserve the feudal system. More generally speaking, I use the term to denote social theory which maintains that there are differences and inequalities between entire groups of people, that these differences and inequalities are natural, and that they should be reflected in social structures of caste or ascription. Antifeminism or patriarchalism is thus a conservative theory of women and men; that is, it claims that there are natural differences and inequalities between women and men which should be expressed in social structures of sexual caste, a sexual division of labor, or what are now referred to as "separate" or "dual" spheres, to indicate that the sexual division of labor appropriately relegates women to the "private" sphere and men to the "public" sphere in a given society.

Of course it is possible to have multiple theoretical/political positions with respect to multiple social structures of inequality and multiple social groups. As I pointed out above, one of the most common sets of political bedfellows is created by the marriage between liberalism and conservatism. In this ideological couple, liberalism as a philosophy of individual difference, individual mobility, equal individual rights, and equal individual opportunity pertains exclusively to certain individuals; other individuals are conceived of as homogeneous groups, naturally different from and inferior to the privileged group and ideally subject to a social system that separates them from that privileged group on an ascriptive or caste basis.

In other words liberal individualism, with respect to upper-class males of intranationally dominant ethnic groups in internationally dominant societies, can be and often is combined with conservatism (castism, patriarchalism, racism, ethnocentrism) with respect to lower classes, women, ethnic minorities, and "Third World" societies. Durkheim, for example, is somewhat ambiguous with respect to class, race, and social groups but is unequivocal in his avowal of liberal individualism with respect to individual men and of conservative patriarchalism with respect to the two sexes, and women in particular.

Others who, like Durkheim, had a conservative answer to the woman question included those who, like him, were liberals on other social questions, but also those who were reactionary, conservative, reformist, or radical toward other social structures and other social groups. For example, in relation to the economic system, some patriarchalists were feudalists, some were capitalists, and some were socialists. Conversely, some feudalists, some capitalists, and some socialists were patriarchalists. The predominant position in Durkheim's milieu, as well as possibly in our own, is Durkheim's own, dual position: some combination of liberalism and conservatism; that is, support for the dual social system, capitalism and patriarchy.[13]

Among Durkheim's forerunners and contemporaries, the combination of liberal capitalism and conservative patriarchalism was most characteristic of the classic liberal Social Darwinism of Darwin and Spencer and the neoliberal sociological theories of Rousseau and Comte. Ironically, however, Durkheim's theory of women, considered separately from his social theory, most closely resembles the misogynist patriarchalism of the socialist Proudhon.

Discourse on "the woman question" in eighteenth- and nineteenth-century Europe can be analyzed in terms of several common themes and issues. The four most salient themes are as follows. First, there are theories about the causes or determinants of particular facts and realities; reasons are established for given conditions or ideals. Second, there are theories about the inherent natural structures, natures, essences, or characteristics of women and men. Third, there are theories about the appropriate social functions, roles, relationships, and systems pertaining to the two sexes. Finally, there are theories about the consequences of various possible social arrangements related to sex roles and relationships.

Among the common issues that recur in classical discourse on the woman question, four seem especially important. First is the issue of women's equal civil rights in the public sphere, most notably the right of suffrage. Second is the issue of women's equal domestic rights in the private sphere, most notably the rights of divorce and ownership of property and income. Third is the issue of women's educational rights, in terms of the extent, nature, and conditions[14] of women's education. Fourth is the issue of women's employment in the paid labor force, "the right to work."

Conservative, patriarchal, antifeminist discourse[15] can be characterized by certain general tendencies with respect to these themes and issues. In the first place, conservatives tended to assign ultimate causality to "nature" and sometimes to "god." They tended to describe women's essential nature or structure as emotional and moral. They tended to delegate to women the social functions of reproduction, domestic labor, child care, and moral education. Finally, they tended to discuss the effects of traditional social sex roles and relationships as positive, beneficial, and advantageous for men, women, children, marriage, the family, society, and/or humanity itself. Conversely, they tended to predict the detrimental, destructive consequences of more egalitarian sex roles and relationships as inimical to the interests of men, women, children, marriage, the family, society, and/or the human species in its entirety.

In general, then, conservatives promoted a social system of separate spheres for the two sexes, with men operating in the social, public, political, economic, and cultural sphere and women operating in the personal, private, domestic, reproductive familial sphere. They based their recommendations on the dichotomous natures, structures, essences, characters, abilities, and capacities of women and men—which natures they perceived as given and unalterable because grounded either in nature or in god. They further substantiated their positions by delineating the necessary and beneficial aspects of traditional sexual differentiation, specialization, segregation, and hierarchy, as well as the contingent and deleterious aspects of greater sexual similarity, convergence, integration, and parity.[16]

I am going to explore the answers of Rousseau, Comte, and Proudhon to the woman question more extensively, since they have the most affinity with Durkheim's answer. Rousseau and Comte are particularly important, because they shared Durkheim's views of society as well as his views of women; furthermore, it is certain that he was quite familiar with their work and positively inclined toward it. Proudhon is particularly important, because despite his views of society, which differed from Durkheim's, their views of women reveal a striking parallel.

Writing in 1762, Jean-Jacques Rousseau[17] believed that "nature" confers certain definite differences on women and men, imbuing them with a dichotomous and complementary set of sexually specific structures that Rousseau refers to as faculties, qualities, characteristics, inclinations, tastes, temperaments, minds, constitutions, natures, or characters. In particular, women are weak, passive, dependent, sexual, and emotional. Thus women have a specific part, destination, contribution, or function in the physical and moral order. "This principle [female weakness and passivity, male strength and activity] being established, it follows that woman was specifically made to please man." It is a "law of nature" that "woman is made to please and to be subjugated to man" (Bell and Offen 1983, 1:44).[18]

Rousseau imagines two possibilities for the future of women, men, and society. In the first instance, women could attempt to emulate men in structure and function. This would have disastrous consequences, Rousseau cautions, for men, for women, and for the human race as a whole. "Woman is worth more as a woman and less as a man. . . . To cultivate in women the qualities of the men and to neglect those that are their own is, then, obviously to work to their detriment. . . . do not make a good man of your daughter . . . make of her a good woman . . . she will be worth more to herself and to us" (1:48). Rousseau, a master of sophistry, admonishes feminists[19] in the following typically unconvincing way. "To advance vague arguments about the equality of the sexes and the similarity of their duties is to lose oneself in vain declamation and does not respond to my argument" (1:46). For his part, Rousseau declaims against feminist objectives with certitude about their impossibility and dire predictions about their repercussions. He opposes the "civic promiscuity" that "mixes the two sexes in the same tasks, in the same work," since it "cannot help but engender the most intolerable abuse." Feminism is "artificial," a "subversion" of nature (1:47).

Conversely, nature's mandates can and should be obeyed: women can and should cultivate and realize their own specific natures as women and specialize in the occupations appropriate to them. Rousseau's reasoning seems to be that because women *are* a certain way, they *should* be a certain way. Thus this is Rousseau's recommendation about the education of women:

> Whether I consider the particular destination of the female sex or observe woman's inclinations, or take account of her duties, everything concurs equally to convince me of the form her education should take. . . . the whole education of women ought to be relative to men. To please them, to be useful to them, to make themselves loved and honored by them, to educate them when young, to care for them when grown, to counsel them, to console them, and to make life agreeable and sweet to them—these are the duties of women at all times, and should be taught them from their infancy. (1:49)

For Rousseau, sexual inequality is natural, not cultural, and therefore its social expression is both reasonable and just. "When woman complains about the unjust inequalities placed on her by man she is wrong; this inequality is by no means a human institution or at least it is not the work of prejudice but of reason" (1:46).

In his *Cours de philosophie positive*[20] Auguste Comte, like Rousseau, invokes "nature" and its corollary manifestations—natural laws, human nature, the nature of all beings, the individual organism, the social organism, universal animal life, universal biology, and the nature of marriage and the family—as the ultimate causal force in sexual dispositions and arrangements. He concludes that there is a radical difference between the two sexes, each of which has its own particular nature. The structural specificity of women is that they are less human than men, being less endowed than men with the characteristic attributes of the human species, notably speculative, intellectual capacity. Thus men are superior, and women are inferior, in "understanding and reason." Conversely, women are more endowed than men with "affective" or emotional and moral faculties, rendering them superior to men in the qualities of "sympathy and sociality" (1:221).

Because of the differentiated structures of women and men, each sex has specialized and complementary functions to perform. In particular, women's function is to "modify" and "moderate" the intellectual, practical, and egoistic activity of men with moral values and social considerations. Despite women's moral and social superiority, however, they are destined to be subordinate to men. According to Comte, "the positive philosophy" will establish that "the subordination of the sexes" is "the principle of marriage and of the family," on the basis of "an exact knowledge of human nature." It will thereby "extinguish the fancies by which the institution is at present discredited and betrayed" (1:220).

For Comte, the "ultimate conditions" of marriage are in accord with "the fundamental principle" of marriage, which is "the natural subordination of the woman"—a culturally and historically universal phenomenon.

> Sociology will prove that the equality of the sexes, of which so much is
> said, is incompatible with all social existence, by showing that each sex
> has special and permanent functions which it must fulfil in the natural
> economy of the human family, and which concur in a common end by
> different ways, the welfare which results being in no degree injured by
> the necessary subordination, since the happiness of every being depends
> on the wise development of its proper nature. (1:220)

In fact, according to Comte the sociological theory of the family consists exclusively of the investigation of two forms of subordination: "the subordination of the sexes, which institutes the family, and that of ages, which maintains it." The "natural economy of the family" consists in the "spontaneous subordination" that constitutes it and then forms the model for "all wise social coordination" (Lenzer 1975, 268–69).

In his *Système de politique positive*,[21] Comte proposed a plan for the reform of patriarchal capitalist ("industrial") society that would resolve "the great moral crisis" it faced (and stave off socialist and feminist challenges) through a coalition of women, workers, and intellectuals.[22] In a very clear articulation of what is now called cultural feminism, Comte emphasized the critical importance of women as the primary agents, and the family as the primary locus, of morality, emotion, spirituality, and social sentiments. According to Comte, "women are the best representatives of the fundamental principle on which Positivism rests, the victory of social over selfish affections" (1:223). Where women represent morality, thinkers represent intelligence and workers represent activity: "Spiritual power, as interpreted by Positivism, begins with the influence of women in the family; it is afterwards moulded into a system by thinkers, while the people are the guarantees for its political efficiency" (1:223).

In *Cours de philosophie positive* Comte had asserted that "spontaneous speculative activity"—in which men are superior to women—is "the chief cerebral attribute of humanity" (1:220). In *Système de politique positive* he reverses himself, to contend that "the most essential attribute of the human race" is "the tendency to place social above personal feeling"—the tendency in which women are superior to men. In "the great object of human life" as well as "the highest attributes of humanity," women thus transcend men (Lenzer 1975, 373–74).

Comte's latter-day elevation of the value of feminine characteristics and the role of women in the reformation of society and in the society of the future does not entail greater political power or economic independence for women. In fact, the moral influence of women, workers, and intellectuals is predicated on their *renunciation* of power and wealth, on their voluntary relinquishment of power and wealth to, respectively, men and capitalists. The progress and perfection of society depend upon the dominance of morality over political and economic life, but it can dominate only if its agents—women—are politically powerless and economically dependent. "In all these matters their influence will be far more effectual when men have done their duty to women by setting them free from the pressure of material necessity, and when women on their side have renounced both power and wealth, as we see so often exemplified among the working classes" (Lenzer 1975, 383).

Women's moral superiority and influence are contingent on political powerlessness and economic dependency in relation to men, whose right to power consists in their possession of utilitarian force in the form of intellectual and physical strength, as workers' moral superiority and influence are contingent on political powerlessness and economic dependency in relation to capitalists, whose right to power consists in their possession of economic force in the form of wealth and the means of production. Intellectual, physical, and material forces are necessary in "practical life" to wrest survival from a perpetually harsh environment. Human progress consists first in the domination of nature by force (industrialism) and ultimately in the domination of force by morality (positivism).

Women are to have a central, even primary, role first in the moralizing reform of industrial society and then, ultimately, in the functioning of the perfect society, organized under the aegis of the positivist religion of humanity. But the centrality and primacy of women does not entail egalitarian relationships with men, structural or functional similarity to men, or participation in the public sphere. On the contrary, women are to be increasingly subordinate, structurally differentiated, and functionally specialized in relation to men, and confined more exclusively to the family.[23] In an irony sometimes characteristic of cultural feminism in particular and dual-spheres feminism in general, Comte maintains that the exaggeration of traditional sex roles and relationships he envisions and endorses would actually constitute "the Worship of Woman."

Durkheim's thinking is in line with Rousseau's in the sense that both advocate separate spheres for women and men in the social order, to reflect their different and unequal "natures" as given in the natural order. The "nature" of women corresponds with the requirements of the private sphere, and the nature of men corresponds with the requirements of the public sphere. Durkheim and Rousseau concur that the public, male sphere is a liberal capitalist political economy, mediated to some degree by "the collective consciousness" or "the general will."

Durkheim and Rousseau have different conceptions of the private sphere and women's work, however. For Rousseau women, as wives and mothers in marriages and families, have important social functions, notably emotional and educational functions serving men and children. For Durkheim the dichotomy between the public and private spheres is also the dichotomy between social and biological structures and functions: women's asocial structure enables them to perform biological functions only; the family is the site of physical activities common to all animals: reproduction, nourishment, hygiene. Similarly, Comte and Durkheim share the view that women and men are structurally differentiated in nature and should be functionally specialized in society, a specialization corresponding to the schism between the private and public spheres. They further agree that the public sphere is and should be the sphere of liberal capitalism, but that liberal capitalism must be reformed to socialize and moralize the egoism of individuals and the materialism of economics. Industrial society requires the positivist religion of humanity; the division of labor in society requires organic solidarity.

But Comte and Durkheim propose significantly different means to substantially comparable ends. For Comte the private sphere is the site of the moral and the social, while the public sphere comprises physical, animal survival and therefore force and self-interest. It is women, within marriage and the family, who will moralize and socialize the men who participate in the amoral, asocial realms of politics and economics.[24] For Durkheim the public sphere contains the amoral, asocial activities of individuals and economics, but it also comprises the moral, social activities of a societywide collective consciousness as well as a multiplicity of occupationally specific collective consciousnesses. Men in the public sphere will socialize and moralize themselves through the state, occupational organizations, and schools. Comte visualizes women leading men as priestesses in the secular, positivist, science/religion of humanity; Durkheim sees only men leading men, as both priests and parishioners in the secular, sociological, science/religion of society.

Rousseau's and Comte's theories of women and society contain unexpected points of convergence and divergence with Durkheim's sexual and social theories. Pierre-Joseph Proudhon's theories of women and society should, logically, differ sharply from Durkheim's, and at first glance they do. Yet on closer inspection they reveal some suggestive points of comparison between the radical socialist and the social reformist. First, Proudhon's "socialism" is actually a theory of universal private property, which has some affinity with Durkheim's defense of private property as a manifestation of "individualism." More provocative and relevant here, however, is the correspondence between Proudhon's and Durkheim's depictions of women and their place in (or outside) society.

Proudhon's theory of women is not complicated by nuance or subtlety. Writing in 1858, he declares it his intention to demonstrate "the PHYSICAL, INTELLECTUAL AND MORAL inferiority of woman" (1:326).[25] Further shunning ambiguity, Proudhon calculates the precise relative "value" of men and women: 3:2 in each of the three categories, 27:8 overall. "Under these conditions, woman cannot pretend to balance man's virile power; her subordination is inevitable. According both to Nature and before Justice she weighs only a third of man; this means that the emancipation being sought in her name would be the legal consecration of her misery, if not of her servitude. The sole hope remaining to her is . . . marriage" (1:330).

The principle of male superiority is "virility": possessing a penis and sperm renders men powerful physically, mentally, and morally. Conversely, the physical inferiority of "woman" is due to her "nonmasculinity," because she "lacks an organ necessary to become anything but a potential adult" (1:327). The intellectual inferiority of "woman" is due to the fact that she "lacks only one thing in order to rival man, which is to produce seed" (1:329). The moral inferiority of woman is due to the fact that "virtue," like intelligence, is "proportional to strength" and consequently her heart, along with her brain and body, all "require fertilization" by a man (1:330). Proudhon concludes his survey of "facts" and "truth" with the following summary of their unalterable natural causes and beneficial social effects: "If Nature wanted the two sexes to be unequal and thereby united according to the law of subordination rather than by that of equivalence, she had her reasons—deeper and more conclusive than the utopias of the philosophers, and more advantageous not only to man, but to woman, to the child, to the entire family" (1:330).

Proudhon's "reasoning" seems bizarre, but Bell and Offen associate it with "an ancient Aristotelian" line of thinking called the "spermatic economy" (1:324).[26] It not only is related to ancient thought but also coincides on certain key points with the patriarchal thought currently under examination. Proudhon grounds sexual difference and inequality in nature and posits a social order that corresponds to the natural order: separate spheres for separate sexes. The social order of sexual specialization is both inevitable, since it is based on natural sexual differentiation, and desirable, since it functions well for all individuals and families and ultimately for society. Proudhon's ideal of universal private property pertains to men only, whose productive activities in the economy must be complemented by the consumptive activities of women in households. The system of private property for men constitutes the public sphere and forms an integral whole with the system of private households for women that constitutes the private sphere.

Even more to the point is the similarity between Proudhon's theory of women and Durkheim's theory of women. This similarity is surprising, given the relative positions of the two men on other social issues, although even this disparity is not as great as one might imagine. Their comparability on the woman question not only is unexpected, it is also unapparent. Durkheim is not so crude or reductionist as to appeal to anatomical differences between men and women to explain their psychological differences. Yet he does appeal to a natural, inherent structural difference that renders women congenitally incapable of accession to psychological, and thus social, equality with men.

The "fact" that women are innately "asocial" appears to be as biologically determined and thus as socially necessary and beneficial as an anatomy that constitutes a destiny. Durkheim ascribes all human qualities to society: individuals (men) are passive recipients of the mental and moral attributes that render them human. The relative degree of socialization determines the relative degree of civilization, or humanness, in a given individual or group. Thus the capacity to be social, to be socialized, to acquire traits that are exclusively collective is decisive in discerning not only the *actual* natural and social state of given individuals or groups, but also their *potential* attainments.

Durkheim is ambiguous about the potential for socialization, and thus for civilization and humanization, of classes, races, and nations: he seems sometimes to impute universal, unilinear evolutionary convergence and sometimes natural, inherent, inviolable hierarchy. With respect to women, however, he is less equivocal. The problem with women is that they are by nature, structurally, "asocial." A natural fact, women's asociality and asociability, underlies another natural fact, women's psychological inferiority to men, which in turn underlies a social fact—the separate spheres of sexual specialization, segregation, and subordination.

17 •

Thus both Durkheim and Proudhon ascribe to a "thing," which men possess and women lack, causal determination of the positive qualities associated with human specificity and civilization. For Proudhon, because men possess and women lack a penis, men possess and women lack the potential potency and virility of sperm—which can be "sublimated" (or "reabsorbed") into physical, intellectual, and moral strength. For Durkheim, because men possess and women lack sociability, men possess and women lack the sole means of acquiring mental and moral propensities—susceptibility to socialization. Durkheim's "sociability economy" is thus the functional equivalent of Proudhon's "spermatic economy," resembling it in form and import if not in content.[27]

Comparing Durkheim with other conservatives on the woman question clearly demonstrates that he was not alone in advocating traditional sex roles and relationships and invoking new, "scientific" arguments for old, stratified social structures. Like other patriarchalists, he viewed women as essentially different and unequal in relation to men. Like other patriarchalists, he believed that social structures of sexual stratification, specialization, and segregation correspond to, reflect, and express natural strictures of sexual disparity, differentiation, and divergence. Like other conservatives, past, present, and future, he found men superior and women inferior intellectually and morally and concluded that men are more, and women less, human.

In one important respect, however, Durkheim's theory of women can be distinguished from other conservative theories of women, and the distinction is a negative one. In general, conservative patriarchalists tended, and still tend, to emphasize sexual difference rather than sexual inequality. They tended, and still tend, to foreground women's unique and valuable natural structures and social functions and to express sexual difference as complementarity rather than as hierarchy. Thus many conservatives—Durkheim's precursors, contemporaries, or successors—extol women's emotional or moral strength as a counterpart to their own physical and intellectual weakness and as a complement to men's emotional or moral weakness. Similarly, they exalt women's emotional or moral roles and glorify their emotional, moral demesne, the family.

More specifically, most conservatives of Durkheim's era or before imputed to women some intellectual, moral, emotional, and/or social capacity and assigned them some intellectual, moral, emotional, and/or social occupation. Most relegated to women responsibility for "socialization," as the education—intellectual and especially moral—of children, and even of men, within the domestic sphere, as well as the duty of providing emotional support for children and for men, again within the domestic sphere. Some even saw women as the primary agents of "socialization" conceived as the mitigation of egoistic, animalistic, survivalistic inclinations by collectivistic, altruistic, socially oriented and socially necessary and beneficial inclinations.

Nineteenth-century conservatism, in other words, dovetailed with nineteenth-century dual spheres or cultural feminism. The two sexes are structurally differentiated and should be functionally specialized, but the difference between their respective structures and functions is not necessarily a difference in value. Whether emotional and moral qualities are inferior, equal, or superior to physical and intellectual qualities and whether unpaid labor in the private sphere is inferior, equal, or superior to paid labor in the public sphere, conservatives and cultural feminists alike have continuously promoted the social value of women's ways and the social value of women's work.[28]

Durkheim, on the contrary, denies women's constitution all human abilities and their actions all human significance. Human mental and moral structures and functions have an exclusively social provenance and are an exclusively male province. Durkheim reduces women to biological beings, relegates them to the family, and reduces the family to a biological entity. As differentiated, asocial structures or cells, women are eternally limited to specialized, asocial functions, primarily biological reproduction. As differentiated, asocial structures or organs, families are progressively limited to specialized asocial functions, primarily biological reproduction.

More precisely, in Durkheim's formulation women's asocial structures and functions place them always, already outside the social organism, and the family's evolutionary trajectory of differentiation and specialization places it increasingly outside the social organism. The social function of women and families is to be asocial—to provide the natural, biological, physical, animal foundation of society. Women and families contribute the physical beings, the male bodies, that are socialized and specialized as individual cells in the collective social organism. Women and families and their functions constitute the prior, external, heterogeneous, material conditions of existence of a male social organism, a masculine collective consciousness, a society of men.

Despite the extremism and absolutism of Durkheim's theory of women, it converges with those of Rousseau, Comte, and Proudhon as a typical example of a prevalent contradiction in liberal capitalist societies. Durkheim combines politico-economic liberalism with respect to some individuals (men in the public sphere) with politico-economic conservatism concerning other individuals (women in the private sphere). The difference between the public and private spheres is not only the difference between social and asocial inhabitants and activities; it is also the difference between caste and individualism, ascription and achievement, tradition and modernity, individual (unspecialized, conventional, labor-intensive, inefficient) forms of labor and social (specialized, scientific, technological, productive) forms of labor, feudalism and capitalism.[29]

The contradictory combination of liberalism and conservatism emerges along different fault lines—lines of sex, race, class, and/or nation—in different theoretical tectonics. And it is a prevalent contradiction in twentieth-century fin-de-siècle liberal capitalism as it was in nineteenth century fin-de-siècle liberal capitalism. Yet it is not now, nor has it ever been, the only theoretical possibility. Examining Durkheim's work in the context of the work of Rousseau, Comte, and Proudhon situates it on friendly theoretical terrain. The work of these four inconsistent liberals is typical in a second respect: their writings equally reflect the presence of an enemy camp on the horizon. What we today call feminism was a force to be reckoned with in the eighteenth and nineteenth centuries, and part of the patriarchal theoretical edifice was constructed in response to feminist maneuvers in theory and practice.

Just as there was a great multiplicity of political positions among adherents of patriarchy, there was a great diversity of political positions among adherents of feminism. I am defining "feminism" as a belief in the equality of potential natural ability between women and men, and thus an advocacy of the equality of actual social treatment for women and men.[30] Among "feminists" thus defined, operating in the theoretical discourse germane to Durkheim, there were representatives of every type of social theory. For example, there were monarchist feminists, Christian feminists, classic liberal feminists, neoliberal feminists, reformist feminists, socialist feminists, anarchist feminists, and utopian communalist feminists.[31]

Landes states it more simply: "Republicanism was just one of several oppositional movements, including socialism and feminism. . . . nineteenth-century French feminism was both republican and socialist" (1988, 171). According to Offen, there was "a broad spectrum of pro-woman advocates whose affiliations ranged from social Catholicism on the right, to revolutionary socialists and syndicalists on the left." For Offen this means that feminist demands were "shaped within what was still a male-dominated political discourse with a fully-developed range of political identities" (in Boxer and Quataert 1987, 178). She discusses how feminists "qualified their feminism with modifying adjectives—bourgeois, socialist, Christian, radical, republican, conservative, syndicalist, and so forth" (1984, 654).

The theorists I have labeled "feminist" tended to support specific social reforms with the intention of improving women's lives. Some of these reforms were relatively "conservative" and were fairly compatible with the traditional sex roles and relationships implicit in the system of dual or separate spheres. Others were relatively "radical" and involved more of a challenge or opposition to traditional sex roles and separate spheres. The more conservative end of the spectrum included equal rights for women within families, as wives and mothers, particularly the right to own property and retain their own earnings and the right to exercise authority over children. These were the most rapidly and extensively enacted reforms. In addition to women's rights as parity with men within legally, religiously, and socially sanctioned official or "legitimate" families, more daring reforms of sexual and reproductive practices were sought. These included the right of both spouses to divorce by mutual consent, the right of mistresses and "illegitimate" children to financial support, the right of all women to birth control, the abolition of prostitution, and the abolition of "separation"—the abandonment by men of their legal wives and children. These proposals met with mixed success.

Women's right to equal education was an ambiguous reform. Some advocated moral education alone for women; some advocated moral and/or intellectual education for women to better prepare them for their traditional roles as wives and mothers; some advocated intellectual education for women for their own self-improvement with no view to any practical application; and of course some advocated intellectual education for women to prepare them to escape and/or augment traditional female occupations through employment in traditionally male occupations. Additionally, Catholics advocated moral and intellectual education for women under the auspices of the church, having ceded the education of men to the secular state. Anticlerical republicans advocated education for women by the secular state to indoctrinate them with republican values and to transfer their allegiance from conservatism and the church to republicanism and the state.[32]

Equal political or "civic" rights for women, including suffrage, constituted a more inflammatory proposal. Some advocated equal political rights for women, with the assumption that this reform would not disrupt the system of separate spheres. Women could become citizens without forsaking women's work. Others, however, saw equal political rights for women as the necessary means to undermine patriarchy: the advancement of women's interests depended on their access to power in the political realm. The opposition to women's political enfranchisement was strong and pervasive. Even left liberal republicans, many women, and many feminists opposed female suffrage out of fear that women would vote conservatively owing to the pronounced influence exerted on them by the Catholic church.[33] The depth and extent of this fear can perhaps be gauged by the fact that French women did not gain the right to vote until 1945.[34]

The most radical reform sought by feminists in the nineteenth century is one that posed (and still poses) the greatest threat to traditional sex roles, the patriarchal family, and the system of dual spheres. This reform, which has yet to be fully accomplished under capitalism, is the right to paid employment in the public sphere, called simply "the right to work."[35] Those who urged the right to work for women encountered opposition primarily from advocates of a sexual division of labor and separate spheres, who viewed the patriarchal family as the optimal means to: (1) realize women's and men's dual natures, (2) to perform a dichotomous set of social functions, and (3) to stabilize heterosexual reproductive relationships—and thus patriarchal society—by creating sexual interdependence within dyads of functionally specialized men and women.

The objections to women's participation in the public, paid labor force were primarily bourgeois objections. They were directed toward a practice that was already prevalent among the working class. In addition to bourgeois resistance, however, there was working-class resistance to paid employment of women, stemming primarily from competition over scarce jobs and low wages. Working-class opponents of women's right to work viewed women as additional, unnecessary, and undesirable rivals, displacing men from a zero-sum, finite set of jobs. The entrance of women into the paid labor force put men's employment in particular jeopardy, since women generally worked for lower wages. In addition to competition from women, working-class men feared the downward pressure on wages resulting from a larger supply of labor, especially if the influx comprised lower-paid workers. Working class opposition to women's paid labor took the form of outright legal prohibitions, a "family wage" for men, and protectionism.

Like antifeminism, feminism in eighteenth- and nineteenth-century France encompassed a wide range of positions on the woman question as well as a wide range of positions on other social questions. Like antifeminism, however, feminism in the classical era contained some broad, general tendencies. In general, feminists protested against the exclusion of women from the rights claimed by men. Some compared women with bourgeois men and sought to have the principles of Right Republicanism, capitalism, and liberalism applied to women. Some feminists compared women with workers and sought the application of the principles of Left Republicanism, socialism, and radicalism to women. All objected to the flagrant inequity of attaining freedom and equality, however defined, for bourgeois, proletarian, and/or slave men but not for women.

• 22

Feminists were acutely aware of the exclusionary, elitist nature of the "universal" "human" rights of "all individuals" as manifested in hegemonic theory and practice. Jenny P. d'Héricourt pointed out this contradiction in 1869: "We find that you accord right to qualities and functions, *because the individual is a man,* and that you cease to recognize it in the same case, *because the individual is a woman*" (1:347; original emphasis).[36] Hubertine Auclert expresses a similar sentiment in 1878: "A suffrage that allows you to exclude from the electoral lists nine million women is far too restrictive to bear the name universal" (1:514).

To argue for the extension of universal, human individual rights to women, feminists found it necessary to explicitly compare women to men, insisting on the similarities that united women and men as opposed to the differences that separated them. Feminists frequently used the phrase "like you" or "like men" and imputed to women attributes that antifeminists claimed were absent or inferior in them. The most disputed characteristic was intelligence, but feminists also ascribed morality, free will, conscience, adulthood,[37] innate freedom and equality, the potential for development, and a soul to women.

In addition to imputing common attributes to women, "like you" or "like men," feminists frequently found it necessary to claim common humanity for them, to claim explicitly that women are human beings, "like you" or "like men." They posited an "identity of species" between men and women and on that basis claimed an identity of rights. Juliette Lambert, writing as Adam in 1858, says pointedly: "When we have forced M. Proudhon to admit that woman is a human being, . . . we will make him admit all that follows" (1:334).

Feminists described the condition of women under patriarchal societal and familial structures in terms that again varied, but not widely. The most common characterization was "slavery," which, along with "serfdom," had great resonance in an era when capitalists and peasants had wrested relative independence and equality from the aristocratic slavery and serfdom of feudalism, workers were attempting to wrest relative independence and equality from the wage slavery and serfdom of capitalism; and slaves were demanding and winning relative independence and equality from feudalist or capitalist colonial forms of slavery. Women were portrayed as "slaves" and "serfs" within a republic and amid free men.

Other terms feminists employed to describe the inequality of women involved similar comparisons with other forms of inequality. Thus there were many references to relations between the sexes as tyranny, despotism, oppression, subjection, exploitation, and subordination, and to men as tyrants, despots, autocrats, feudal lords, capitalists, and slaveholders. Most delineated the cause of sexual inequality simply as the domination of women by socially and physically more powerful men for their own selfish interests, accompanied by their familial, political, and economic reinforcement—and cultural rationalization—of this domination. Most delineated the solution to sexual inequality as the bestowal by men, or the conquest by women, of equal familial, political, educational, and employment rights for both sexes.

Several writers managed to evoke something of the specificity of women's oppression, such as those who discussed the way it cut across class lines, rendered women members of a single social category, and gave them a common interest in more egalitarian sex roles and relationships. Nelly Roussel was a turn-of-the-century French counterpart to cultural feminists and birth-control crusaders in the United States. She foregrounded the common oppression of all women, particularly through "forced" maternity, the denigration and debilitation attendant on maternity, and the predominance of a "masculine" culture of conflict and violence. "All of us can declare war on today's society, for all of us are more or less ruined, our bodies, our hearts, our consciences brutalized by its laws." She anticipated radical feminism by referring to all women, especially mothers, as "martyrs" or "the eternal victim" and advocating the refusal to reproduce, and/or the socialization of children to reject men and male society (2:134–36).

Ironically it was a man, Charles Fourier, who emphasized the role of the sexual division of labor as the primary cause of sexual inequality. Under this system, domestic labor and child care are performed inefficiently by individual women, who are rendered economically dependent on individual men in private households. He proposed the socialization of these forms of labor, along with waged work for women and communal living, to promote universal freedom and equality.[38] According to Bell and Offen, "He seems to have been the first thinker to write about the centrality of women's domestic responsibilities to their subordination in the family" (1:143).

The methods and primary objectives of feminists varied. However, feminists were fairly unified in their predictions of the negative consequences of continued sexual inequality and the positive effects of improvements in women's condition. Women's liberation and sexual equality were obviously seen as vital to women's interests; their happiness was contingent not on the maintenance, revival, or exaggeration of traditional sex roles, but on their reform or transformation. Feminists also stressed the advantages that would accrue to men, children, families, and sexual-reproductive morality through the greater freedom and equality of women.

More generally, feminists felt that sexual inequality and the effective servitude of women prevented the complete realization of revolutionary ideals and promises of freedom and equality. Many also viewed the condition of women as a crucial practical factor in the success or failure of any social movement or order. Another common feminist theme was the contribution women could make to each sphere of social life, to the solution of social problems, and to society and humanity in general through their active participation, as a doubling of the force or power of men and/or as a contribution of unique qualities possessed only or primarily by women: for example, compassion. As opposed to antifeminists, then, feminists posited a real ultimate unity of interests rather than an apparent immediate conflict of interests between women, men, the family, morality, society, humanity, and feminism.

Set against this background, Durkheim's theory of women seems more retrograde than when compared with those of other antifeminists. It is particularly difficult to comprehend the predominance, in Durkheim's time and our own, of inconsistent liberalism—of the advocacy of universal human rights for a particular subset of human individuals. Yet it seems more reasonable to compare Durkheim's antifeminism with the feminism of his liberal, capitalist confreres (and consoeurs) than with the feminism of his socialist adversaries. Conversely, to render an accurate view of the full extent and array of possible political positions available to Durkheim, it seems necessary to at least sketch the position at the opposite end of the spectrum from Durkheim's extreme antifeminism and neoliberal support of capitalism.

The feminists whose other political positions were most like Durkheim's include other classic liberals and neoliberals who accepted capitalism and wanted to either conserve or reform it. They include Mary Wollstonecraft, the marquis de Condorcet, John Stuart Mill, Harriet Taylor Mill, Marianne Weber, Jules Ferry, and Charlotte Perkins Gilman.[39] John Stuart Mill seems especially relevant. *The Subjection of Women* was reviewed positively in the Comtist-positivist *Revue Philosophique* in 1870 by Edouard de Pompéry. The work was also endorsed by Jules Ferry, French minister of public instruction and prime minister, in an 1870 speech that reappeared in 1893 in a book of his speeches and essays (1:392, 405–6, 438–42). Comte was interested enough in Mill's theories of women that he entered into an epistolary debate with him (Thompson 1976, 189–210).

It is ironic that Durkheim, the founder of sociologism, and Comte, the "father of sociology," both invoke natural and biological determinism to explain women and sexual difference. Similarly, it is ironic that both social theorists, who are liberals with respect to men, are conservatives with respect to women and thus constitute inconsistent liberals but consistent proponents of separate spheres.[40] In contrast to Durkheim and Comte, Mill proves consistent, both as an adherent of social determinism and as an adherent of liberalism, in applying these theories to women as well as men.

Condorcet also seems particularly relevant as a theorist who was influential and parallel in relation to Durkheim, with the signal exception of the woman question. Durkheim lectured on Condorcet, among other precursors of social science, and Lukes presents Mauss's account of those lectures. According to Mauss, Durkheim had a " 'keen admiration' " for Condorcet, "whose writings he 'knew thoroughly' and whose influence on Saint-Simon and Comte he noted" (Lukes 1985, 277). Durkheim credits Condorcet as a "brilliant" (though prescientific) member of the historical lineage of sociology.

Writing a hundred years before Durkheim and maintaining, like Durkheim, a belief in separate spheres, Condorcet nonetheless takes feminist positions on a number of issues. First, he believes that women are human beings, enough like men to constitute part of one species. Because of the common humanity of women and men, he endorses equal rights for women: "Now the rights of men result only from this, that men are beings with sensibility, capable of acquiring moral ideas, and of reasoning on these ideas. So women, having these same qualities, have necessarily equal rights. Either no individual of the human race has genuine rights, or else all have the same" (1:99).

More specifically, Condorcet maintains that there is "an entire equality" of intelligence between women and men and that women have an equal right to education. If social structures are to conform to nature, reason, and justice, education must be sexually egalitarian and sexually integrated (1:82): "*Instruction should be the same for women and men*" (1:79; original emphasis). Furthermore, Condorcet views women as primarily responsible for the moral education of children and men and thus in some sense morally superior to men. For Durkheim women are neither intelligent nor moral beings, since they are not social beings. Atypically, Durkheim ascribes women's characteristics to their nature rather than ascribing their nature to their social structures and situations.

Condorcet, however, anticipates Mill's arguments by eighty years, claiming that differences and inequalities between women and men express differences and inequalities in their social conditions, not the reverse. For example, "superiority of intelligence" among men could be "the necessary result of difference of education" (1:99). Similarly, Condorcet responds to the contention that women lack a sense of justice: "It is not nature, it is education, it is the manner of social life, which is the cause of this difference" (1:100–101). If women have different political sensibilities and interests than men, it is because of their different, and subordinate, position in society.

Condorcet compares the subordination of women under patriarchy to the subordination of capitalism and capitalists under feudalism and the subordination of slaves under slavery. All are forms of tyranny, all are justified in the name of utility, "the excuse and pretext of tyrants," and all are contingent rather than necessary (1:101). Furthermore, all forms of inequality are harmful to society, since "inequality necessarily introduces corruption" and is associated with barbarism rather than civilization (1:102). The maintenance of sexual inequality would conserve the "spirit of inequality" in women and men alike even in a republic, whereas equality is not only an individual right but a social imperative. "In the institutions of a free nation, all should tend toward equality not only because this is a right of men but because the maintenance of order and peace urgently requires it. A constitution that established political equality will neither endure nor promote tranquility if it is mixed with institutions that maintain prejudices favorable to inequality" (1:82).

Condorcet's social theory resembles Durkheim's on the "man question" if not on the woman question. Jeanne Deroin's socialist feminism is located at the opposite end of the political spectrum from Durkheim's capitalist patriarchy. Her arguments are quite typical of feminist arguments, and her experience epitomizes feminist struggles in nineteenth-century France: she ran for office before women could vote, she engaged in a bitter debate with Proudhon, she was imprisoned, and she finally died in exile. She advocated women's rights in the name of liberty, equality, fraternity, truth, justice, law, religion, morality, intelligence, socialism, Christianity, the interest of society, the salvation of humanity, women's equality with men and their difference from men, women's status as half of humanity and half of society, women's special function as mothers of children, and the special quality of "woman" as "mother of humanity": "maternal love" or "humanitarian maternity."

Deroin holds up sexual inequality as "the negation of the principles of liberty, equality, and fraternity." Inequality is a barrier to all social ideals. The regeneration of society will require the reunification of humanity, "but first we must put a stop to the struggle between the two halves of the grand human family, man and woman" (1:262–63): "The abolition of the privileges of race, birth, caste, and fortune cannot be complete and radical unless the privilege of sex is totally abolished. It is the source of all the others, the last head of the hydra" (1:263). Privilege of sex is "the worst one of all" (1:248).

The consequences of maintaining the subjection of women are manifold and profound. Women remain "helots" and "slaves" within a republic. The country is "deprived of the services of its daughters" (1:247–48). Notably, only women, imbued with maternal and humanitarian love, "can rise above these party and sectarian hatreds that divide men, and can teach everyone how fraternity should be practiced." Women must intervene and help to transform "this politics of violence and repression, which produces only deep hatred and which causes all suffering and social misery" (1:262).

Deroin appropriates the doctrine of sexual difference to diametrically opposite effect than does Durkheim: "It is precisely because woman is equal to man, and yet not identical to him, that she should take part in the work of social reform and incorporate in it those necessary elements that are lacking in man, so that the work can be complete" (1:281). She argues from sexual difference to include women in the public sphere. And she returns from sexual difference to sexual equality: "To refuse to woman the right to live the social life is to commit a crime against humanity" (1:281).

"Woman" has an equal right to help form the laws that govern "society, of which she is a member" (1:288). Furthermore, since women constitute half of humanity and society, it is not only right but necessary to include them in governance: "A Legislative Assembly composed entirely of men is as incompetent to make the laws that rule a society of men and women, as an assembly composed entirely of privileged people to debate the interests of workers, or an assembly of capitalists to sustain the honor of the country" (1:280–81).

The ultimate consequence of denying freedom and equality to women is women's enmity, and hence the destruction of the culpable regime. Writing, with Pauline Roland, from the prison of Saint-Lazare to the United States Women's Rights Convention of 1851, Deroin explains the failure of the French Revolution of 1848.

> The darkness of reaction has obscured the sun of 1848. . . . Why? Because the revolutionary tempest, in overturning at the same time the throne and the scaffold, in breaking the chain of the black slave, forgot to break the chain of the most oppressed of all of the pariahs of humanity. . . . the fundamental law . . . is still based upon privilege, and soon privilege triumphs over this phantom of universal suffrage, which, being but half of itself, sinks on the 31st of May 1850. (1:287–88)

Deroin's conception of social reform, social organization, social solidarity, socialism, and the religion of humanity, unlike Durkheim's, is characterized primarily by unity between the working class and women, by collective ownership of the means of production, and by sexual equality and integration.

Perhaps the most celebrated socialist feminist in nineteenth-century France was Flora Tristan, who, like Jeanne Deroin, focused on the similarity between women and workers and advocated the alliance of women and workers. According to S. Joan Moon, Tristan was the first French reformer "to synthesize feminism and utopian socialism by securing sexual equality through the self

emancipation of the working class" (1978, 21). She connected amelioration of the conditions of women with amelioration of the conditions of workers by promoting the education of women, especially working-class women. The problems of the working class were caused by the vicious cycle of "poverty and ignorance, ignorance and poverty"—a cycle that could be broken through the only kind of education the working class could afford: the free education of children and men, in the home, by educated women.

Tristan argued that "the education of man in general and man of the lower classes in particular depends on the education of woman" (1:213). Thus she could enlist working-class men in the cause of feminism in the name of ideals such as human rights, "the progress of humanity," and "universal well-being," but also in the name of their own self interest and their own advancement. She could claim that "the law that enslaves woman and deprives her of an education also oppresses you, proletarian men" (1:215). In 1843 Tristan provided an anticipatory feminist corrective to Marx and Engels's 1848 slogan, "WORKING MEN OF ALL COUNTRIES UNITE," with her own slogan, "UNIVERSAL UNION OF WORKING MEN AND WOMEN" (1:215).

Tristan also anticipated, and in effect advocated, the double day and the second shift for working-class women (as Betty Friedan did more than a century later for middle-class women). If working-class women could be educated, they could "improve the intellectual, moral, and material condition of the working class" by serving as "skillful workers, good mothers . . . and . . . moralizing agents in the life of the men" (1:213): "Then, you, men of the lower classes, will have as mothers skillful workers who earn a decent salary, are educated, well brought up, and quite capable of raising you, of educating you, the workers, as is proper for free men" (1:214).

Women had been enslaved throughout history, Tristan argued, and "all the misfortunes in the world result from the neglect and contempt in which woman's natural and inalienable rights have so far been held." She viewed the Declaration of the Rights of Man as a proclamation of "the neglect and contempt of the new men" for women and warned that women's eternal protest had finally attained critical mass, because "the exasperation of the slave has reached its peak" (1:213). The time was ripe for feminist revolution, and Tristan extended an invitation to working-class men to be on the side of history.

Text and Context

Attempting to situate Durkheim in his historical context, like reconstructing his theories of women and society, is not an exact science. Nevertheless, contextual analysis can supplement textual analysis and enrich understanding of Durkheim's texts and his times far beyond the understanding gained by simply "reading Durkheim." Durkheim's description of and reaction to the realities and discourses of his era distort as well as reveal their "referents." We can do more than merely conjecture about the differences between Durkheim's words and Durkheim's world by exploring other words about the same world. Articulating the structure of his social theory against the discursive and material structures of his own temporal and spatial reality, as well as against the discursive and material structures of our own temporal and spatial reality, illumines relations among things, among theories, and between things and theories in Durkheim's era and between the words and things in his era and the words and things in ours.

The first effect of this work of contextualization is the realization that Durkheim's theory of separate sexual spheres of ability and activity was not necessarily or inherently as antifeminist as it might appear today and in the Anglophone political discourse. Offen, among others, challenges us to rethink the relationship between feminism and the traditional sexual division of labor, particularly in the nineteenth century and particularly in continental Europe. This challenge is richly rewarded by an exploration of the discourses on women that she and Bell have meticulously compiled. The discoveries attendant on this exploration dispel many condescending myths about the place of women in their shadowy material and discursive past.

The first myth to be dispelled is the myth of women's historical passivity in relation to real and theoretical structures. Our foremothers participated actively in "public"—productive and political—theories and practices, in addition to their active participation in "private" productive and political theories and practices, in the "second sphere" of domestic labor and familial relations on which the "first sphere" of paid labor and "social" relations has always rested. The second myth to be dispelled is that everyone in the nineteenth century was a feminist, that all nineteenth-century feminism was the same, or that all nineteenth-century feminism resembled the particular form of feminism endorsed by each of us today. The historical discourse on women was characterized by a wide gamut of feminisms and antifeminisms, which were additionally characterized by a wide gamut of relationships with other theoretical-political positions on other theoretical-political questions. Durkheim's theoretical constructions have extremely complex relationships with "other" constructions, the extremely complex discursive and material structures of his milieu, and cannot be "simply" dismissed as "simply" antifeminist.

Conversely, these exploratory discoveries dispel the myth that Durkheim, in answering the woman question, was "a product of his times." Although not everyone in nineteenth-century Europe was a feminist and not all nineteenth-century feminists opposed dual spheres, feminism existed in many forms, as did feminist opposition to dual spheres, and feminist positions were found in many combinations with other social theories. Feminism and feminist opposition to dual spheres were viable, if not mainstream, reactions to the social structures and social changes Durkheim described. Durkheim could have chosen and defended these positions and remained well within the parameters of contemporary social theory. In fact, given his daring, "radical" rebellion from the hegemony of classic, laissez-faire, utilitarian, individualistic liberalism, he could have improvised and advocated feminism, including its most "extreme" forms, in the same iconoclastic and powerful way.

The question is not in what way Durkheim was a product of his times. The question is why Durkheim was so committed to patriarchy. To some extent this is to ask why so many liberals were and are so inconsistent. In fact, Durkheim's inconsistent combination of liberalism with respect to men and conservatism with respect to women is quite consistent with the predominant inconsistency of liberalism in general. "Liberalism" is actually a compound of liberal individualism vis-à-vis some individuals and conservative racism, sexism, classism, nationalism, and ethnocentrism toward other individuals. This heterogeneous theory and practice reflects the uneasy relationship between an ideology of individual ability, agency, mobility, meritocracy, and equal opportunity and a reality of multiple de facto caste systems and perpetual structural inequalities.

Durkheim's real inconsistency, the aspect of his chauvinism that is incompatible and contradictory in relation to his own theory and that of other liberals, capitalists, and patriarchs, is the extremity and absolutism of his theory of women. By describing women as structurally asocial, he denies them all mental and moral abilities and activities. He denies women humanity and condemns them eternally to the netherworld of primitive, animal, physical, biological structures and functions inside/outside a modern human, mental, and moral universe. Men are cells in the social organism. Women are merely organisms.

Why does Durkheim formulate such an extreme and absolute answer to the woman question, rivaled only by Proudhon's in its sheer misogyny? I think the answer lies in his theory about the division of labor in society. He is a fierce proponent of individual specialization, not as a means to greater economic productivity, but as a means to greater social solidarity—a way to integrate and regulate increasingly atomized and anarchic individuals. Interdependence is for Durkheim the answer to the social question of excessive individualism, to the modern problem of egoism and anomie. His definition of "society" is interrelated, solidary individuals, and his definition of marriage is "conjugal society."

Mechanical solidarity, the solidarity of resemblance, was obsolete in sexual and social relations. Modern society, and modern conjugal society, had to be created, and they had to be created through organic solidarity, which is based on interdependence, which is based on the division of labor. The social division of labor would ultimately unite individuals in mutual dependence and organic solidarity. The sexual division of labor would ultimately unite men and women in mutual dependence and conjugal solidarity. Durkheim had a fear, a fear of socialism, and he had a desire—a desire to wed owners and workers eternally in the wage contracts of capitalism. Durkheim's social fear and desire had their counterparts in sexual fear and desire. Durkheim had a fear, of feminism, and a desire, to wed men and women eternally in the dual spheres of patriarchy.[41]

Chapter **2**

DESCRIPTIONS

OF

WOMEN

• Durkheim's oeuvre is clearly characterized by its silence on the subject of women—by the conspicuous absence of women in its many pages. Of course the repression of women by a text, their expulsion/expurgation, exclusion/exile from the printed page, constitutes a theoretical *treatment* of women in and of itself. To some extent Durkheim's theory of women is the very invisibility of women in his theory.[1] Durkheim does formulate a "positive" theory of women, however, in the very specific sense that women do assume a certain presence in his work; they materialize and take form in his writing, ghettoized though they may be within it.

Durkheim theorizes women in the following places: passages in *The Division of Labor in Society* and *Suicide;* an article on divorce; and review essays in *L'Année Sociologique* under the heading "Domestic Organization," includ-

A different version of this chapter appeared as "Durkheim's Women: His Theory of the Structures and Functions of Sexuality," *Current Perspectives in Social Theory* 11 (1991): 141–67.

ing the subheadings "The Family," "Marriage," and "Sexual Morality" (the index in the English compilation of Durkheim's contributions to *L'Année* reads: "Women. *See also* Family; Marriage"); as well as passim under the heading "Criminal Sociology." It is surprising and particularly revealing that in most of his review essays, and in the surviving lectures of his course on the family, even Durkheim's family sociology systematically omits any mention of women.[2]

Durkheim pays negligible attention to women within his sociological theory. The observations he does make about the sexual difference appear scattered and incidental. Nevertheless, his work does in fact contain a coherent, consistent, systematic sociological theory of women. This theory is more latent than manifest, more immanent than articulate. It must be reconstructed. As the structure of Durkheim's sexual sociology emerges, the importance of sexual theory to his social thought, as well as the importance of Durkheim's thought to sexual theory, becomes evident.

The importance of sexual theory to Durkheim's social thought has several aspects. Foremost is that, despite the scarcity and dispersion of its manifestations, he does evince a specific, structured, and multifaceted theory of women. They are not completely absent from his sociological thought or from his theoretical portrait of society. Like an unresolved problem underlying a neurotic symptom, women are un/important in that they are never Durkheim's exclusive focus, but their image recurs throughout the expanse of his work.

In piecemeal fashion, then, Durkheim theorizes women. He theorizes their presence or being, as women's/woman's "nature," giving this the same reified, determinant necessity that all his morphological anatomies and ontological models assume. And he theorizes their position or situation in society as women's/woman's "place," deriving this from the dual causal imperatives: woman's nature and society's needs.

The natures of women and men are different and specific. This sexual differentiation bears both the eternal finality of nature and the inexorable inevitability of evolution. Society requires and utilizes both the difference itself and the specific skills of each sex. The sexual division of labor is thus doubly determined: by nature, through the natural natures of women and men and the progressive differentiation thereof, and by society, through the social functions these natures and these differences serve.

These pronouncements are presented by Durkheim as disinterested science, as objectively excavated fact, as methodologically unearthed reality. They are presented as the indisputable discoveries of an undisturbed and undisturbable "new world," which is merely that dimension of the old world unseen by untrained eyes. In themselves these "scientific observations" have a conservative import. Although he denies being a "reactionary" because he questions every institution, Durkheim admits to being a "conservative" because he sagely recognizes the immutability of the social/natural facts he uncovers.

Traditional sexual roles and relationships are thus naturalized and written in stone, through Durkheim's descriptive dissection of male and female natures and through his descriptive demonstration of the general social good effected by the corresponding sexual division of labor. There is a natural substructure, the sexual difference in nature. This is a decisive reality. And there is a social superstructure, the sexual division of labor. This is a contingent reality.

As a scientist, the authorial/authoritative position, the auteurial/artistic point of view, that Durkheim constructs for himself is outside this complex structure, faithfully sketching its outline, passively representing its configuration, honestly rendering its reality. This structure, and this stance, is parallel to the multilevel structure comprising the relationship between the division of labor in society and organic solidarity, as Durkheim elaborates it in *The Division of Labor in Society*.

The morphological substructure of modern society is the differentiation of individuals. This necessitates a moral and institutional superstructure of the organic rather than the mechanical type. "Necessitates" is a crucial word, designating a critical relationship. A moral order of individual difference and interdependence, a solidarity based on the occupational similarity of individuals and the occupational difference of groups, is *required* by the naturally emergent specialization and individualization of society. It is expressive of society's nature, and it is essential to society's functioning. This means that it is automatic. It also means that it is arbitrary. Because it is compatible with—reflective/expressive of—the division of labor, organic solidarity *will* exist, and for the same reasons it *should* exist. Durkheim, the neutral scientist, simultaneously describes and advocates its existence.

In exactly the same manner, Durkheim, standing apart from the sexual division of labor, can simultaneously endorse it scientifically by positing its inevitability and endorse it scientifically by positing its desirability. Its inevitability and its desirability rest on the same base: the sexual division of human nature, or at least Durkheim's scientific depiction of it. Whether naturally determined or socially chosen, the sexual division of labor is *necessary*. It does not matter whether it occurs spontaneously or is adopted deliberately. You mustn't fight Mother Nature: you *can't* fight Mother Nature, and you *shouldn't* fight Mother Nature. This is Durkheim's scientific/political message. He implicitly delineates the futility of tampering with sex roles, of "messing with" nature's creation. His science asserts simultaneously that this intervention is impossible and that it is undesirable.

This whole science of sex roles is itself the foundation of another superstructure: Durkheim's politics of sex roles. The science is covertly and implicitly—scientifically—political. The politics is overtly and explicitly—expressly—political, and implicitly but impressively scientific. Durkheim's science constitutes a set of admonitions and injunctions against concerted social action and social change. His politics constitutes a set of admonitions and injunctions about the form concerted social action and social change should take. Based on his scientific formulations about the natural differences between men and women and the socially functional division of labor arising out of that difference, Durkheim formulates both a response to feminism and a vision of the natural and ideal future of sex relations.

Durkheim's assertions about women can be disentangled into two categories: statements about reality, or description, and statements about ideality, or prescription. This chapter focuses on description. Here I reconstruct Durkheim's ontology of sexuality, deferring his prescriptions, as well as his contradictions, to subsequent chapters. Within the world of reality as he conceives it, Durkheim produces theories about the nature of women, or their putative *structure,* and about the role of women, or their putatively proper *function.*

The Structures and Functions of Sexuality

Structures of Sexuality:
The Differential Natures of Women and Men

The nature of women, according to Durkheim, is that they are natural, in a pejorative sense. For Durkheim, society is the progenitor of all that is mental and moral. Women are fundamentally, inherently, intrinsically asocial; they are asocial by nature and are therefore part of nature rather than part of society.[3] For Durkheim women are the weaker sex; they are weaker mentally and morally because they are the extrasocial sex. They are by nature excommunicated from the collectivity that collectively generates and individually receives both ideas and ideals. They are therefore left behind men in a state of nature, which for Durkheim is a lowly, pathetic, and inferior state.

Society, the source of the intellectual and ethical—in other words, of the human psyche itself—represents the ultimate good in Durkheim's eyes. Therefore the value of a particular society or group can be measured in terms of its degree of socialization, or civilization. In fact the very humanity, or humanness, of a society or group is relative and is specifically related to its level of sociality, or socialness. Thus women's distance from society is the very mark of their distance from humanity: to Durkheim women are uncivilized primitives at best, and nonhuman animals at worst.[4]

This theme is introduced in *The Division of Labor*, specifically in the section on suicide. The suicide rate is seen to be a function of the "degree of civilization" of social groups. Accordingly, women's low suicide rates reflect their low degree of civilization. "It is the same with the sexes. Woman has had less part than man in the movement of civilization. She participates less and derives less profit. She recalls, moreover, certain characteristics of primitive natures" (1933, 247). The difference between men and women is comparable to that between "lower societies" and modern society (250).

The same theme is developed in *Suicide*. There it is seen that women "have no great intellectual needs." The sensibility of "woman" is "rudimentary": "As she lives outside of community existence more than man she is less penetrated by it; society is less necessary to her because she is less impregnated with sociability. She has few needs in this direction and satisfies them easily. With a few devotional practices and some animals to care for, the old unmarried woman's life is full. . . . very simple social forms satisfy all her needs" (1951, 215–16). Women are comparable to "lower," "primitive" societies, with their "simple" social inclinations, which "need little for satisfaction."

Since men are viewed as social animals and women are viewed as natural animals, Durkheim believes that there is a sexual difference in sexuality itself. The very sexuality of men becomes social while the sexuality of women, naturally, remains natural. Women's sexual needs have "less of a mental character" than men's because "generally speaking her mental life is less developed": "These needs are more closely related to the needs of the organism, following rather than leading them and consequently finding in them an efficient restraint. Being a more instinctive creature than man, woman has only to follow her instincts to find calmness and peace. . . . her desires are naturally limited" (1951, 272). Women are naturally protected—that is to say protected by their very nature, which is natural—from the "disease of the infinite," from infinite sexual desire. Because this sexual disease is social and mental in origin, it afflicts males exclusively. Similarly, women are naturally protected, as natural creatures, from suicide. "If women kill themselves much less often than men, it is because they are much less involved than men in collective existence; thus they feel its influence—good or evil—less strongly. So it is with old persons and children" (299).

In general, women are relatively immune to social forces. Their position outside society provides shelter from all influences of collective, cultural origin, including harmful ones. According to Durkheim, they escape social impulses not only to anomie and suicide, but also to crime. Women do not share in men's life of crime, nor do they experience a socially induced increase in crime with the advance of civilization. "This is because the causes are social, and women . . . by not participating as directly as men in the collective life, submit less to its influence and experience less of its various consequences" (1980, 409).

If shelter from social problems is the consolation women enjoy because of their Otherness, there are drawbacks. First, although women are immune to the negative effects of divorce (notably suicide), they are also immune to the positive effects of marriage. The existence of divorce does not exacerbate female suicide rates precisely because of the "general law" which holds that "the state of marriage has only a weak effect on the moral constitution of women." The "woman" to which Durkheim frequently refers "stands somewhat beyond the moral effects of marriage," just as she stands beyond the reach of society in general (1978a, 247).

The second disadvantage is that since women are not truly socialized and do not really internalize social impulses, their natural, asocial impulses lie very close to the surface. Thus, for example, criminal behavior emerges in widows, whose crime rate is "intensified." The family is the sole social bond and constraint that women experience. Furthermore, it is a superficial social force—with respect to women, truly an external constraint. Therefore when women, persistently and essentially unsocialized, are detached from the family through widowhood, they readily succumb to their natural inclination to crime: "She is less resistant to the shock of events as soon as she is subjected by force of circumstances to more direct involvement in the action" (1980, 414).

This is consistent with Durkheim's position that women are no less criminal or immoral than men; they merely lack criminal opportunities owing to their distance from social life. "Woman kills herself less, and she kills others less, . . . because she does not participate in collective life in the same way. . . . she merely lacks as frequent opportunities, being less deeply involved in the struggle of life. . . . Moreover, she is far from having the same antipathy to these two forms of immorality. . . . Whenever homicide is within her range she commits it as often or more often than man" (1951, 341–42).

The higher crime rate among widows thus "proves" that "woman's moral sense is less deeply rooted than man's." It substantiates the "truth" that "woman's nature is less strongly socialized than man's" (1980, 414). Women are, in effect, social castratas. They are devoid of negative social pressures, such as those conducive to crime and suicide. Conversely, they are devoid of positive social pressures, such as those that deter crime and suicide. When women are good, they are good for all the wrong reasons. When women are bad, they are bad owing to natural causes.

The antagonism between the sexes is the third deleterious effect of the asocial nature of women. Since men are social and women are not, men and women constitute two diverse and opposed interest groups within society. In fact the sexual differentiation is the only deep internecine division Durkheim admits to in the family of man; the sexual opposition is the only fundamental conflict of interest he admits in the society formed by a unity of individuals. The antagonism of the sexes, he says, originates in the fact that "the two sexes do not share equally in social life. Man is actively involved in it while woman does little more than look on from a distance. Consequently man is much more highly socialized than woman. His tastes, aspirations and humor have in large part a collective origin, while his companion's are more directly influenced by her organism" (1951, 385).

Given this sexual difference of interest, each social phenomenon must have two contrasting effects: one on men and one on women. "It cannot simultaneously be agreeable to two persons, one of whom is almost entirely the product of society, while the other has remained to a far greater extent the product of nature" (1951, 385). Marriage, for example, is beneficial with respect to social beings—to men and their society. Therefore it is necessary. But though it is functional, and therefore inevitable, it is at the same time detrimental with respect to "the other half"—to natural beings, women.

There is, according to Durkheim, a "flagrant . . . psychological inequality" that radically separates women from men (1951, 386). Having declared the *human* to be equivalent to the *social,* he defines women as less social, as asocial, relative to men. The logical deduction is that women are not human, or are subhuman, relative to men. Ultimately, the social/asocial distinction is the difference in "structure" or "morphology" that differentiates women and men. Like any radical morphological difference, it suggests a difference in classification, a categorical difference. Women and men have different and unequal natures; they are different and unequal species.

The difference between men and women is a fact of nature. It is also a product of evolution. Durkheim believes that the structural differentiation of men and women progressively increases throughout human history. The primitive condition is one of structural similarity between the sexes. The opposition between social men and natural women "was originally less marked than now" (1951, 385). Sexual homogeneity is characteristic of both childhood and "the beginning of human evolution" (1933, 57).

The specific process by which sexual differentiation emerges and advances is the gradual development of men, combined with the stagnation or regression of women. Men and women begin history equivalently, as simple, primitive, instinctual natural creatures. Men diverge from women to become something different; to become social, mental, and moral human beings. Men become social and society becomes male in the same movement, a movement in which women do not and cannot participate. Men evolve into men, become civilized and humanized, leaving women behind in species limbo as primitives.

As opposed to eternally simple women, men step over the threshold into modern, superior, specifically human complexity. "As his thought and activity develop, they increasingly overflow these antiquated forms. But then he needs others. . . . he is a more complex social being" (1951, 215–16). The thought and activity of women remain undeveloped; women remain in the realm of antiquated forms, which for them never become antiquated. Women are forever simple and asocial beings. They are forever young, representing humanity in its infancy, its natural state. Women represent the animal in man and the physical dimension of mankind. Men represent the humanity in man and the psychic dimension of the human animal. Women are trapped in the biological as men are enmeshed in the social. The structure of women, or "the female form," constitutes "the aboriginal image of what was the one and only type from which the masculine variety slowly detached itself" (1933, 57).[5]

The growing difference between men and women reflects the general direction of human evolution. Just as primitive individuals resemble each other, so primordial males and females resemble each other. Advanced, modern society is characterized precisely by progressive, infinite individual and sexual differentiation. It has taken "the work of centuries" to produce the "flagrant" "psychological inequality" that distinguishes men from women. But this evolutionary work is not finished. "The female sex will not again become more similar to the male; on the contrary, we may foresee that it will become more different" (1951, 385). "And evolution does seem to be taking place in this direction. Woman differs from man much more in cities than in the country; and yet her intellectual and moral constitution is most impregnated with social life in cities" (386).

Functions of Sexuality:
The Occupational Specialization of Women and Men

The difference in structure that divides women and men from each other also destines them to a sexual division of labor. As male and female structures are differentiated, so male and female functions should be specialized. The contrasting natures of men and women should find expression in sex-segregated

39 ▪

occupations. "By constitution, woman is predisposed to lead a life different from man" (1933, 264). Furthermore, Durkheim asserts that "we have no reason to suppose that woman may ever be able to fulfill the same functions in society as man" (1951, 385).

Functional specialization is the fate of the sexes as well as of individuals. But it is with respect to sexual specialization that Durkheim moves beyond generalities. The nature of women suggests the nature of work that corresponds to their inherent abilities, as the nature of men suggests the nature of work suitable to them. The specific structures of men and women specifically determine their proper respective functions. Abstractly speaking, the sphere of activity to which women are "predisposed" by "constitution" is "affective" activity. Conversely, men are constitutionally predisposed to other, nonaffective functions—notably to intellectual functions. "One might say that the two great functions of the psychic life are thus dissociated, that one of the sexes takes care of the affective functions and the other of the intellectual functions" (1933, 59).

The preeminent sphere of affective functions is of course the private, domestic world of the family. It is "precisely . . . women's role" to be wives and mothers, "to preside over this interior life . . . family life" (1978c, 143). The family, in fact, is "unexcelled as a territory for feminine activity" (1980, 209). The family is only the best expression of femininity, however. Durkheim observes women "coming out" or emerging from interior, private life and entering exterior, public life. There too women specialize in affective functions, leaving intellectual functions to men. Outside the home women, characteristically, participate in "artistic and literary life."

The potential and partial entry of women into the public sphere, in suitably feminine roles, is only a manifestation of the historical tendency to ever greater functional differentiation between the sexes. As evolution produces increasingly disparate male and female structures, males and females occupy increasingly disparate functions. Like the sexual difference in nature, the sexual division of labor develops progressively over time, becoming particularly pronounced in advanced, modern society. Primordially, the sexes are alike in function as well as in nature. Structural similarity is accompanied by "functional resemblances": "In these same societies, female functions are not very clearly distinguished from male. Rather, the two sexes lead almost the same existence. There is even now a very great number of savage people where the woman mingles in political life . . . men's lives . . . war" (1933, 58). But civilization entails specialization at the sexual as well as at the individual level. In "modern times," "sexual labor is more and more divided. Limited first only to sexual functions, it slowly becomes extended to others. Long ago, woman retired from warfare and public affairs, and consecrated her entire life to her family. Since then, her role has become even more specialized. Today, among cultivated people, the woman leads a completely different existence from that of the man" (1933, 60).

The Structures and Functions of the Family

The progressive evolution of the sexual division of labor is very closely associated with the historical development of the family. Durkheim describes a complex process of simultaneous institutional and sexual specialization centered on the family. The first aspect of that process is, as noted, the definition of the family as the sphere of activity proper to women: the specialization of women in the family and the specialization of men in extradomestic endeavors. There are two additional, interrelated dimensions of familial differentiation. First is the external dimension, or the family's institutional structure. Second is the internal dimension, or the family's organizational structure. Typically, Durkheim sets up a contrast between the "primitive" structure of the family and its "advanced" or evolved, modern, and superior structure.

The History of the Family: External Differentiation and Specialization

The primitive family is part of the collective type of society and obeys the principles of mechanical solidarity. This primitive form entails familial extensity; domestic "collectivism" or "communism"; domestic despotism and a total absence of individuality; and a coherent combination of uterine descent and matriarchy. Matrilinearity is associated with matriarchy: women in matrilineal society are relatively prestigious and privileged. Matrilinearity is also associated with the primitive, incohesive form of the conjugal family. Sexual relations are primarily nonmonogamous, and women are relatively independent from their husbands. Women's primary orientation is to their natal family rather than their conjugal family, and it is the natal, matrilineal family that is the collective, despotic mass where property is held, communally, and individual identity is absorbed and lost.[6] This is the theory behind Durkheim's statement about the primitive nature of female privilege: "A mind with a revolutionary bent, especially if given to socialism, will be swept along by its passion for the weak and by its tendency to come to their defense, and will judge the varieties of families according to the way they treat women. But the privileged situation of women, far from being a sure index of progress, is sometimes caused by a still rudimentary domestic organization" (1978b, 213).

The entire pattern of the primitive family is disrupted by the advent of the testamentary form of inheritance. The will symbolizes the emergence of an individual identity within the family, in the person of the father. At first the father is only a figurehead, an individual personification of the communal family. But eventually the communal family is displaced by the patriarchal family. Finally, the apex of the evolutionary process is what Durkheim calls "the conjugal family." It is the product of a dual trend: the continuous contraction and emergence of the family, culminating in a circumscribed and distinct unit. The conjugal family is the ultimate, completely differentiated form of the family. "The law of contraction or progressive emergence has been verified. Invariably we have seen emerging from primitive groups increasingly restricted groups which tend to absorb family life completely" (1965a, 536).

The conjugal family represents a final contraction, "a contraction of the paternal family." As such, it is characteristic of "the most civilized peoples of modern Europe."[7] The patriarch appears within the extended communal family, at first as its representative. Then the extended communal family becomes the patriarchal family, which is also extended, but to a lesser degree. Finally the patriarchal family constricts until only the smallest possible family unit remains, containing only the conjugal couple and their children. This family, commonly referred to as the nuclear family, is detached from the rest of society and from many of its previous functions. It is at once differentiated and specialized with respect to its external, institutional milieu: differentiated from the extended family, the clan system, and so forth, and specialized in noneconomic activity. The conjugal family is confined to the few members who are directly involved in procreation and to the few functions that are not eventually appropriated by occupational institutions.

The History of the Family:
Internal Differentiation and Specialization

The externally differentiated and specialized conjugal family is also internally differentiated and specialized. "The married couple, at first lost in the crowded family, detached itself, became a group sui generis that had its own physiognomy and its special set of rules" (1980, 236). Durkheim acknowledges that there are societies in which "the occupations of the sexes are in fact the same" within the family, familial types "where all the adults play the same role and are on the same plane of equality." Nonetheless, he implies that this is unnatural: "It appears quite natural that the different members of the family should have duties, that is to say, different functions according to their degree of relationship" (1951, 264–65). Intrafamilial specialization is not inevitable, then. When it occurs it reflects the innate differences among family members that "make possible the division of labor" and that would otherwise remain latent. Special-ization is natural because it makes use of these "natural differences" and because it corresponds to them.

In addition to being natural, the domestic division of labor shares the other merits of the general division of labor, the division of labor in society. It is, first, an efficient method of organization. But more important for Durkheim is the fact that it is a method of organization. Society becomes a complex, structured organism, instead of an amorphous, impotent mass, through the interrelation-ship of differentiated individuals. Similarly, Durkheim believes, the family can, through internal differentiation, emerge from its primitive, mechanical state into the advanced, desirable state of organic solidarity. And this is the final merit of specialization. It provides a superior method of organization, and the specific type of organization it engenders is characterized not by lesser but by greater unity.

43 ■

The object of *The Division of Labor* was to demonstrate that specialized individuals are actually more highly integrated than identical individuals—that organic solidarity is more solidary, and therefore more social, than mechanical solidarity. The division of labor, whether it exists in society or the family, is a superior, natural, efficient, unifying, and particularly social form of organiza-tion. Like the general society, and indeed like all of nature, the familial society inevitably repeats the universal evolutionary process.

In relation to its social milieu, the family contracts in both structure and function until the supreme form, the microcosmic and institutionally spe-cialized "conjugal family," emerges. The conjugal family or "conjugal society" undergoes internal differentiation parallel to the differentiation of both institu-tions and individuals in society at large. Durkheim does not elaborate the details of the internal specialization of the family, with two exceptions. First, as noted, he finds that the inherent nature of women predisposes them to confine their activities to the domestic milieu, while the inherent nature of men pre-disposes them to move outside it. However, he also believes that men have a crucial familial function to fulfill. Although men remain largely external to the family, once inside it they specialize in the exercise of power. Durkheim ex-plicitly defends patriarchy and suggests that, with modifications, it is appropri-ate to the modern family. In modified form, patriarchy is an important dimen-sion of familial organization and the domestic division of labor.

While providing what he believes to be scientific support of patriarchy, Durkheim acknowledges the feminist repudiation of it. Yet he acknowledges the feminist position only to refute and dismiss it. In reviewing a work by Marianne Weber, he says: "Her entire theory rests on the principle that the patriarchal family has brought about a complete enslavement of women. In its absolute form, the proposition is most disputable" (1978c, 143). Instead of the "unfair" tendency to "downgrade unjustly" the Roman system of patriarchy, for example, Durkheim proposes that "it is as vain to attack it as it is to defend it. It is enough to understand it and to see what justifies it in the social context where it is to be found" (1980, 178).

Presumably Durkheim's description of the Anglo-Saxon system of patriarchy demonstrates a fruitful, scientific, and objective "understanding" as opposed to the futile alternatives: an unjust attack or a superfluous defense. "It was, then, a relationship implying supremacy and protection on one side and submission and self-sacrifice on the other—without, however, anything degrading being attached to this subordination" (1980, 254).

Durkheim gives varying accounts of the social reasons for, and historical causes of, patriarchy. Originally patriarchy emerged as "family communism" was dismantled, individualized, and organized through the introduction of the last will and testament. The evolution of patriarchy was tied to the evolution of testamentary inheritance and adoption: "This is also the evolution from which came the authority of the family's father, for the right to make a will is one of the principal points involving the patria potestas" (1980, 177).

> The authorization to make a will . . . was to run up against the principle of family communism—a principle it negated. . . . the family was induced to incorporate within the person of the *paterfamilias,* to relinquish into his hands, the powers it held at the start. Accordingly, the father came to be invested with almost limitless power. It was not by virtue of the respect that individual personality would have inspired from then on; the fact is that he was, literally, the family personified. He was their agent. His authority stemmed from that of the family group and was entrusted to him, as it were, by delegation. (1980, 228–29)

The limitless power of patriarchy, then, originated as a domestic form of representative democracy. The family *incorporated* itself in the person of the father; it *relinquished* its power to him; it *invested* him with power; it *personified* itself in him; it took him as its *agent;* it *entrusted* absolute authority to him by *delegation.*

Durkheim is more vague in his explanation of the investiture of communal family power specifically in the male individual. To some extent he apparently takes it for granted. But occasionally he overtly acknowledges the masculinity of patriarchy. "But this movement has profited only the masculine segment of humanity. The chiefs of individual families have always been men. . . . this hegemony has been necessitated by the very conditions of life. Notably, the importance of military functions explains the social primacy attributed to the stronger sex" (1978c, 142). This explanation is uncharacteristically perfunctory for Durkheim. In addition, it contrasts with another, equally perfunctory, explanation given elsewhere: "Because of age, because of the blood relations he has with his children, the father is the one who exercises the authority in the family, an authority constituting paternal power" (1933, 264).[8]

Typically, Durkheim is more concerned with social and historical functions than with social and historical causes. The structure of patriarchy, in his view, has many functions. Historically, it facilitated the dissolution of the primitive family type, matriarchal communism. Patriarchy created an individual, the patriarch, who assumed an identity distinguishable from the family collective. Initially the individual patriarch was only a symbol of that collectivity, but ultimately he paved the way for its individuation/dissolution. "The constitution of the patriarchal family corresponds to a first movement in the direction of individuation" (1978c, 141). Equally or more important, is the fact that patriarchy provides a means of organizing and unifying the individuals so differentiated—a higher, more complex, and stronger unity than that of familial collectivism. The family was "transformed" from the disorganization of communism to the structure of patriarchy. "Instead of remaining overextended, it became organized" (1980, 228). In order "to organize itself," family communism abdicated its "monarchical" power and submitted itself to "the entire organization authorized by the father" (1980, 236).

This form of organization proved particularly vital. Durkheim repeatedly cites the "strength" of the marital and familial bonds in Rome, the "close unity" of the Roman patriarchal family (1980, 256). In Roman society "conjugal intimacy was already very great" (1980, 220). Durkheim indicates that "never was the bond of matrimony stronger than in Rome, never was the union of man and wife more fully regarded as an inviolate partnership throughout the whole of life" (1980, 292). Furthermore, "the strongest and the most intangible family bonds that have ever existed" are "those which issued from the patripotestal authority (*patria potestas*) and which placed the child under the domination of the father" (1980, 205–6).

The position of children under patriarchy is brought to the fore in this last quotation. This position represents part of the specificity of ancient patriarchy and part of the reason for its subsequent adaptive modification. The Roman form of patriarchy became outmoded for several reasons. First, as the statement above indicates, it represented an autocratic domination of the father over the children, and specifically over the sons. This domination eventually conflicted with the very individualism that patriarchy inaugurated. In fact, in the vast majority of his work on the family, it is the nature of the father/son relationship, and its transformation over time, that preoccupies Durkheim. Second, the patriarch exercised dominion over an extended family. The patriarchal family was more constricted than the primitive communal family/clan, but still more extensive than the ultimate and ultimately reduced family type, the conjugal family. Patriarchy had to be transformed because it gave the father too much power over his sons and power over too many persons.

The "law" regulating the evolution of the family was its continual contraction, culminating in the emergence of the conjugal form. Patriarchy, the transitional moment in this evolution, itself had to evolve and eventually adapt itself to the restricted, marital family. This new form of patriarchy, corresponding to the new nuclear family, Durkheim calls alternatively "conjugal authority," "marital authority," and "family authority." All these terms refer to the transferal of family power from the father of an extended family to the husband of a contracted family and to the substitution of the spouse (wife) for the child (son) as the primary object of that power. Just as the conjugal family is "a contraction of the paternal family," so conjugal authority is a contraction of patriarchal authority. Durkheim describes this dual evolution of family structure and family power in the following passage: "Marital authority was only one aspect of paternal authority. But to the degree that the second declined, the first emerged and established itself independently and more strongly. The husband had right. in his capacity as husband" (1980, 236).

Durkheim's explanation for the fact that "conjugal" authority devolves exclusively on men is as cursory as his explanation for the male "hegemony" in patriarchy. At one point he even, atypically, dismisses the need for an explanation: "For reasons easy to understand, the husband was placed in charge—all of which necessarily put the wife in a subordinate position in relation to him" (1980, 260). Elsewhere he simply states that "conjugal" authority is vested in the husband because it is. "The authority of the latter comes not from natural supremacy but from the fact that the community he forms by his association with his wife is in need of a chief and he is that designated chief" (1980, 218). Only slightly more satisfying is a suggestion that the husband's particular role within the family confers and even consists of a certain degree of power. Privileges accorded to the husband "would pertain to the special role the husband plays in the household, to the duty he has to protect and to direct the wife—in a word, to the overall rights and obligations which make up marital prerogatives" (1980, 250).

A central aspect of the power of the husband in conjugal society is the fact of joint conjugal property, which reflects the structure of the newly differentiated nuclear family. As the conjugal family replaces the communal family, property is held in the marital unit rather than the consanguinal unit. It is shared by the spouses rather than separately owned in their respective natal clans. This common conjugal ownership both mirrors and solidifies the unity of the conjugal couple (1980, 251). But in addition, it constitutes a marital activity that needs to be administered. And for Durkheim it is unquestionably the male who will administer it.

Ostensibly, "conjugal authority" consists primarily in the husband's administration of the joint conjugal property and as such is not particularly coercive or oppressive. It is merely an administrative relationship of convenience, a bureaucratic arrangement. This system originated in medieval Europe. "In the Middle Ages, although the wife was subordinate to the husband, she was nevertheless considered to be his partner: The husband was the administrator of the common patrimony, not the master of the situation" (1980, 293). In the conjugal family "the property of both spouses forms an indivisible whole" that "the husband administers." This is part of the "special role" played by the husband, part of the foundation of his special rights and privileges.

The fact that the spouses of the conjugal family have a "common patrimony" forms the economic context of one of Durkheim's explanations of male rights cited above. With the emergence of joint conjugal property, it becomes necessary "to organize its administration and to fix the role of each" (1980, 260). The establishment of joint marital property involves "a certain economic subordination of the wife to the husband," a certain "relative dependence" (1980, 261). It is because "the economic interests of the two spouses are merged by the regime of joint ownership" that "it is necessary that the indivisible society thus formed have one head. There results from this a certain subordination of the wife" (1980, 218).

Of course, with respect to conjugal authority, Durkheim is characteristically more concerned with necessary and beneficial effects or functions than with causal explanations. And the functions of conjugal authority are very similar to the functions of the patriarchal authority it derives from. Conjugal authority constitutes a strong form of organization for the conjugal family. Its greatest function, however, is that it creates a strong unity within the conjugal society. Durkheim sees it as "inevitable" that "at least at a given moment in history" the tightening of matrimonial and familial bonds requires and produces the "subordination of the wife to her husband."

The subordination of the wife, which originates in the husband's administration of joint conjugal property, is "needed for good conjugal discipline and for the shared interest of the household" (1980, 218). This same subordination can be understood as "a means of unifying the conjugal society" and as "indispensable to domestic discipline" (1980, 260). In fact, for Durkheim "*this subordination*"—the subordination of the wife under the husband, which is the converse of the conjugal authority of the husband over the wife—"*is the necessary condition of family unity*" (1980, 209; emphasis added).

■ 48   The structure of the relationship between women and men parallels the structure of the relationship among individuals in society. Primitively it is a relationship of similarity and equality. At the zenith of its evolution, it is structured by the sexual division of labor and by inequality. The sexual division of labor, or the divergence of functions performed by each sex, is first and foremost a split between domestic and extradomestic activity, with women specializing in affairs of the heart and the hearth. Beyond the division that consecrates women to family functions, there is an intrafamilial division of labor in which men specialize in the exercise of familial power. This begins as patriarchy and ends with the contraction of the patriarchal family and the expansion of individual autonomy (specifically, that of the male offspring) as conjugal authority.

The Social Functions of the Sexual Division of Labor

These structures of differentiation and power, the sexual and familial divisions of labor, not only are inevitable products of evolution, they are also desirable. They are desirable because, as structures, they perform certain necessary and beneficial functions. In the first place, the difference in activity (functional difference, division of labor) between men and women expresses the difference in nature between men and women (structural difference, division of ability). The two sexes *are* systematically different from each other, and so for the good of individual women and men as well as in the social interest of efficiency, they *should* engage their talents appropriately, which is to say in different ways.

This correspondence of sex-specific ability with sex-specific occupations is important to Durkheim. Thus the first function of the sexual/familial division of labor—the social expression of natural difference and structural/functional correspondence—has inherent value and significance. But it is the second function that takes precedence and constitutes the crucial social contribution of sexual specialization. This is the function of creating sexual and familial solidarity.

Just as the division of labor in society produces a new, higher form of social solidarity, so the division of labor in marriage and the family produces there the transcendent, organic form of solidarity, an invincible solidarity based on interdependence. For Durkheim, solidarity is the highest social and moral good, the raison d'être of society. And interdependence is the supreme basis of solidarity, the raison d'être of the division of labor. "The most remarkable effect of the division of labor is not that it increases the output of functions divided, but that it renders them solidary" (1933, 60–61).

Durkheim specifically cites conjugal society as an example of the connection between the division of labor and organic solidarity: "Precisely because man and woman are different, they seek each other passionately. . . . In short, man and woman isolated from each other are only different parts of the same concrete universal which they reform when they unite. In other words, the sexual division of labor is the source of conjugal solidarity" (1933, 56).

The sexual division of labor has advanced throughout history: from affecting "only sexual organs and some secondary activities" it has been extended "to all organic and social functions." In this progression, it has developed "concomitant with conjugal solidarity" (1933, 57). In primitive or "savage" societies where "female functions are not very clearly distinguished from male" and where "the two sexes lead almost the same existence," conjugal solidarity is found to be "very weak." Marriage among these primitive, androgynous savages "is in a completely rudimentary state" (58). By contrast, "as we advance to modern times, we see marriage developing." This is due to the fact that "sexual labor is more and more divided": "Limited first only to sexual functions, it slowly becomes extended to others. . . . Today, among cultivated people, the woman leads a completely different existence from that of the man" (1933, 60).

In fact, Durkheim notes that the universal division of labor "has been carried to the last stage" between the sexes: there are faculties "completely lost by both" (1933, 401). Among these same cultivated, sexually differentiated people, conjugal solidarity "makes its action felt at each moment and in all the details of life." It intimately and intricately binds together specialized male and female beings who are "incomplete" and "mutually dependent" (61).

The sexual division of labor is functional, since it engenders solidarity in sexual society. But more fundamental than this, according to Durkheim, the sexual division of labor actually creates sexual society ex nihilo. Marriage in essence is a society. It is potentially and ideally a bond that is "holy," that has "sanctity," "moral validity," and "a social function"—a "moral communion." In other words, it is a microcosmic replica of society itself. The fact that the conjugal association "always becomes more powerful and cohesive as history advances" means that its "moral unity" increases over time. Marriage is at heart a mental and moral, not a sexual or economic institution. Like any society, it is a mental and moral fusion of physically distinct individuals.[9]

Marriage consists primarily of "intercourse" that is "other than sexual," and the economic relations of marriage merely reflect the social and moral web that is its real significance. "If public conscience represents marriage as a source of morality, so to speak as a sacrament, it is because the spouses conceive in their minds the formation of a moral unity [*société morale*] of exceptional significance, and not simply a physical identity" (1980, 247). Marriage is a moral unity, a moral society, a moral identity conceived in the minds of its members. It is a mental, moral, and social union, not merely a physical union. Even sex is in some sense social and moral. "The conjugal act (and more generally, the sexual act) is not religiously neutral, but brings into play forces which are sacred and consequently formidable" (1980, 270).

It is in this sense that the sexual division of labor not only strengthens but actually constitutes the society of men and women: "Permit the sexual division of labor to recede below a certain level and conjugal society would eventually subsist in sexual relations preeminently ephemeral. If the sexes were not separated at all, an entire category of social life would be absent" (1933, 61). The sexual division of labor is a specific instance of the general division of labor in society. The function of the division of labor, in general, "consists in the establishment of a social and moral order *sui generis*" (61).

"Its role in all these cases is not simply to embellish or ameliorate existing societies, but to render societies possible that without it would not exist. Through it, individuals are linked to one another. Without it they would be independent. Instead of developing separately, they pool their efforts. They are solidary (1933, 61)."

Chapter **3**

PRESCRIPTIONS

FOR

WOMEN

- **The Rejection of Feminism**

    Durkheim rejects feminism as "an unconscious movement." Feminism, he says, "deceives itself when it formulates the details of its demands." This is because feminism and its demands are premised on a belief in sexual equality, which Durkheim does not share. For example, he dismisses as "personal ideas" and "generalities" an author's contention that women are equal to men. "He has not examined or discussed in detail the reasons why certain thinkers—among them some women . . .—have argued against the feminist movement" (1980, 253). The reason Durkheim argues against the feminist movement is that he deems sexual equality to be primitive, unnatural, and dysfunctional.

A different version of this chapter appeared as "Durkheim's Response to Feminism: Prescriptions for Women," *Sociological Theory* 8, no. 2 (1990): 163–87.

Sexual Equality Rejected as Primitive

Durkheim discredits and denounces sexual equality by describing it as "primitive." If men and women resemble each other and perform similar functions, if they exist side by side and in egalitarian power relations, then sexual relations are prehistoric. Such an arrangement is elementary, undeveloped by the natural evolution that differentiates men and women into specialized structures and functions, organizes and stratifies their relations. If men and women are identical, integrated, and equal, they exhibit only the crude, primordial social relations of mechanical solidarity. Durkheim specifically rejects each form of sexual equality—structural resemblance, functional similarity, proximity, and parity—as a primitive phenomenon.

Sexual similarity, or "homogeneity," is essentially a manifestation of individual or social immaturity. In terms of individual development, it is characteristic of childhood. Historically, it belongs to "the beginning of human evolution" (1933, 57). In the beginning there are no men and women; there is a unitary, unisex "one and only type," the "aboriginal type." In "primitive" societies men and women are structurally indistinct. In addition they are functionally indistinct: "anatomical resemblances are accompanied by functional resemblances": "In the same societies, female functions are not very clearly distinguished from male. Rather, the two sexes lead almost the same existence. There is even now a very great number of savage people where the woman mingles in political life . . . men's lives . . . war" (1933, 58). Sexual homogeneity, Durkheim concludes, is inherently "savage" or "primitive." He expresses and condenses this theory in the term "primitive homogeneity."

According to this same scheme, sexual proximity, or integration, is characteristic of simple, unsophisticated sexual roles and relations. Primevally, the two sexes "constantly blended their existence in the most intimate acts of life." Conversely, sexual segregation is a modern phenomenon, an "advanced" feature of society "today." From the late Middle Ages to the present, the two sexes form "two distinctly separate worlds."[1]

Finally, Durkheim delegitimizes sexual parity, or equality in power relations, by associating it with the "primitive" family structure. According to Durkheim, women have relative power, prestige, privilege, and autonomy in matrilineal society. He views matrilinearity, in turn, as both obsolete and crude. Matrilinearity is part of a configuration of inferior family characteristics that includes weak conjugal relations and a weak conjugal family. Generally, women enjoy relative self-determination owing to the system of female descent and to the laxity of marital bonds, even promiscuity, that system entails. Specifically, women have independence from their mates owing to a persistent and primary orientation toward the natal clan. Women do not belong to their husbands because they continue to belong to their birth families. This theory of history is encapsulated in the following statement: "The privileged situation of women, far from being a sure index of progress, is sometimes caused by a still rudimentary domestic organization" (1978b, 213). Female privilege, like sexual homogeneity and sexual integration, is definitionally "primitive."

Under primitive conditions, neither society nor the family is organized according to a division of labor. The coexistence of women and men is characterized by identity: resemblance, similarity, proximity, and parity. Of course this mechanical social and sexual solidarity is backward: it is simple, inefficient, and very weakly integrated. According to his evolutionary scheme, Durkheim believes that, like individuals, the two sexes *will* eventually be differentiated, specialized, segregated, and stratified and that they *should* be.

Sexual Equality Rejected as Unnatural

Durkheim opposes sexual equality because he believes it is a primitive phenomenon. His evolutionary organicism, in turn, reflexively equates the primitive with the inferior. Beyond its alleged primitivism, however, Durkheim finds sexual equality objectionable because it is unnatural. This position can be discerned in the following dense passage from *The Division of Labor:* "By *constitution,* woman is *predisposed* to lead a life different from man. . . . It appears quite *natural* that the different members of the family should have duties, that is to say, *different functions*" (1933, 264–65; emphasis added). Sexual difference and inequality are endorsed by nature: by the difference and inequality inherent in the "constitution" of each sex. Sexual difference and inequality are "natural" and therefore inevitable and ideal. Sexual equality is essentially unnatural and therefore essentially unlikely and undesirable.

Durkheim states his case more clearly in this polemical passage from *Suicide:* "As for the champions today of equal rights for woman with those of man, they forget that the work of centuries cannot be instantly abolished; that *juridical equality cannot be legitimate so long as psychological inequality is so flagrant*" (1951, 386; emphasis added). The psychological inequality of the sexes is a natural fact. It is the product of centuries of natural evolution, at the end of which it is extreme, flagrant. This natural sexual inequality should be expressed in social institutions. It "cannot" be eliminated, and therefore it should not be contradicted. To do so would be illegitimate, a violation of natural law.

Sexual Equality Rejected as Dysfunctional

The social expression of sexual inequality is natural but also, naturally, it is socially functional. Among other things, a hierarchical sexual division of labor provides a means of organizing the family. Durkheim's work is premised on the idea that the functional, collective needs of society and its institutions, such as the need for familial solidarity, take precedence over any antisocial, private needs of individuals. This is because he believes that in the final analysis the interests of society and the true interests of individuals are essentially identical. Individuals should make short-term sacrifices for the good of society because in the long run what is good for society is good for its dependents.

Durkheim repeatedly argues this position with respect to the family. One of his reasons for rejecting sexual equality is the deleterious effect it would have on this institution, and subsequently on society as a whole and all its individual members. A "total equalization of wife and husband" is cited as a menace to the family, as a factor that would "compromise the organic unity of conjugal society and of the family" (1978c, 143). Durkheim undoubtedly views equality as a short-term and misguided "individual" objective that should be subordinated to the long-term, genuine general interest. The good of the individual is actually and ultimately to be realized through the family and society. Equality is only an individual/antisocial and apparent/false need that disorganizes/destroys the family and thereby both society and the individual. This analysis is at the root of the "uneasiness" that feminism and sexual egalitarianism cause Durkheim. This is what makes the woman question a "difficult question": "The equality of the two sexes will be achieved only if the woman blends herself more and more into external life; *but then how will the family be transformed?*" (1980, 305; emphasis added).

The Appropriation of Feminism: Separate but Equal

Durkheim is not content to merely condemn feminism. In his view feminism is ideological, but it is based on a genuine perception of genuine social problems. Therefore his theoretical strategy is compromise, and his theoretical tactic is redefinition. He redefines feminism until it is unrecognizable and indistinguishable from reformist patriarchy; then he claims that he too is a feminist. "I do not feel that I am a reactionary," he says (1978a, 240). He even appears in some instances to advocate equality for women. However, Durkheim's definition of equality has much more in common with the doctrine of separate (and different) but equal than with most feminist definitions of equality.

Thus Durkheim concedes that the feminist movement is more than "a short-lived vogue." But he counters that it "deceives itself when it formulates the details of its demands." He seems to accept the movement for women's equality, but he insists on specifying the nature of that equality as one that is both possible and desirable within his theoretical framework. He would provide the necessary correctives to the deceptive details of feminist demands. Concerning feminism, Durkheim is more equivocal than egalitarian.

The Doctrine of Separate but Equal:
Sexual Structures and Functions

Durkheim's most important construction/destruction of the concept of sexual equality is found in the following passage: "*Nonetheless, it is quite true that woman should seek for equality in the functions which are commensurate with her nature*" (1980, 296; emphasis added). Women can be "equal" to men, but only on the condition that they are different from men. Sexual equality does not preclude sexual specialization but depends on it. Durkheim intimates what the specific and differential but equal functions of women will be, in this cautionary statement: "*The future role of the woman can, however, only be determined by understanding her role in the past, and the functional conditions in the parameters of which that role has differed*" (1980, 296; emphasis added). Thus Durkheim not only defines/destroys sexual equality by equating it with sexual difference, but also inverts the feminist ethos by equating it with a hypostatization of traditional sex roles.

The foundation of Durkheim's sexual theory is his "scientific description" of the structural differentiation of men and women. This structural differentiation, which is primary, natural, and inevitable, is itself the foundation of functional specialization, of the sexual division of labor, which is derived, social, and contingent. According to the theory of structural sexual differentiation, men and women are intrinsically, essentially, different. Each sex has its own specific morphology, its own specific "constitution" or "nature." There is a male psychological structure, and there is a female psychological structure. Human nature is sexed, which is to say that there is no human nature. "Human nature" does not exist because it is bifurcated into masculine nature and feminine nature. Whereas: "By constitution, woman is predisposed to lead a life different from man" (1933, 264). Therefore: "woman should seek for equality in the functions which are commensurate with her nature" (1980, 296).

Durkheim's formulation of functional specialization according to sex is both descriptive and prescriptive. Given the "fact" that men and women have different structures, and given the "fact" that the nature of these structures is determinate, it becomes possible to specify the functions that naturally *do* and *should* correspond to each, masculine or feminine, structure. In particular, the "asocial" nature or "constitution" of women "predisposes" them to nonintellectual functions, a lower, "other" category that Durkheim euphemistically labels "affective." Whereas "intellectual work" remains a generalization, affective work is defined with precision. Affective functions and family functions are one and the same.[2]

Family functions constitute a role within the "functional parameters" of women's traditional role throughout history. In fact the "future role of the woman" *will* and *should* be identical to "her role in the past." Durkheim descriptively "observes" the "fact" that "long ago, woman retired from warfare and public affairs and consecrated her entire life to her family." He determines, both descriptively and prescriptively, that: "*women's role . . . is precisely to preside over this interior life . . . family life*" (1978c, 143; emphasis added). And he concludes, descriptively/prescriptively, that: "*the family is unexcelled as a territory for feminine activity*" (1980, 209; emphasis added).

Family Strength as Women's Salvation:
The Identity of Interests Linking Females and Families

The structural functionalist model of sexual relations is based on the assumption/ascertainment that the sexes are naturally different. This natural structural difference produces and determines functional specialization. The specific assignment of sexual roles is based on the assumption/ascertainment that women are naturally suited for nonintellectual, "affective" functions. The differential constitution of women predisposes them to a differential role. The specific nature of the female constitution predisposes them to a specific role: the family function. Because women are different, they should seek equality in different functions. Because women are asocial, affective, animal—physical, biological— they should seek equality in familial functions.

Finally, since women should specialize in familial functions, they should seek equality within the family, through familial strength. Having established that women's place is in the home, Durkheim easily argues that women's status is determined by their status in the family and by the status of the family in society. Therefore he recommends that to elevate their own status, women should concern themselves with elevating the status of the role and institution in which they naturally specialize. The first aspect of women's equality is the equal fulfillment of their particular—different, specific, feminine—nature. This is accomplished through women's specialization in the family. The second aspect of women's equality is the equal prestige of their particular—different, specific, feminine—occupation. This is accomplished through society's strengthening of the family and glorification of the wife and mother.

Women are accorded rank, prestige, and privilege in several social structural circumstances. As indicated above, they have high status in primitive societies and families. Yet it is clear that Durkheim rejects these social and familial forms and the type of sexual equality they engender: similarity, proximity, and parity, including the relative power and autonomy of women. These societies, these families, and these sexual equalities are "primitive," "rudimentary," preevolutionary. They are inferior, relatively less adapted, relatively less functional structures. It would be retrograde to advocate a return to or an approximation of this backward state.

According to Durkheim, however, it is also possible for women to attain equality in modern society, on two conditions. Modern equality is the formal equality that women derive through the full realization of their special nature. Therefore the first absolute condition for civilized sexual equality is that, in accordance with natural law, modern women are specialized and situated in the family. But modern equality is also the reverence and respect that women derive through the high social estimation of their special function. Therefore the second absolute condition is that the modern family is strong and sacred in society.

Durkheim exhorts women seeking equality to devote themselves to the family and to attach their own social destinies to the social destiny of the domestic milieu. "It is the woman's place in the family which is presumed to have determined her place in society. The principle is indisputable" (1978c, 140). Women are more or less "well treated" depending on the importance of their social function. This means that their welfare is served by increasing the importance of women's role within the family and by increasing the importance of the family within society. Feminists should strive not to modify, dismantle, or undermine the traditional family, but to consolidate it. Women sabotage themselves when they sabotage the family. "Everything which can contribute to the weakening of the organic unity of the family and of marriage must necessarily have the effect of eliminating this source of feminine grandeur. . . . The respect shown her, a respect that has increased over historical time, has its origin mainly in the religious respect which the hearth inspires" (1978c, 144). If the religion of the family were to be attenuated, "women would thereby be diminished."

Women's rights disrupt the family: the two concerns are opposed and mutually exclusive. Therefore, since the fate of women is tied to the fate of the family, women's rights are actually antithetical to women's best interests. Any gain due to their "conquest" of rights "claimed on their behalf" would be offset by "important losses" (1978c, 144). Women's status or "position of rank" is not achieved through independence: "Nothing seems to us more contestable than this" (1980, 303). Women's status is achieved through the status of woman's place, which is the home, and the home is not a place of liberty.

In general the status of women is determined by the relative strength and unity of the conventional nuclear family. For example, a close marital relationship, a marked intimacy between husband and wife, tends to "reinstate the status and the authority of the mother in the family" (1980, 275). In the opposite case, the dyadic core of the conjugal family is only a loose association, "a precarious union of two beings," each free to separate and each with "his or her own circle of interests and preoccupations." Under these conditions the religion of the family is vitiated and imperiled, and women are consequently "diminished" (1978c, 144).

The status of women has several specific components. Most concrete is their "juridical condition." The juridical condition of woman, Durkheim says, "depends on her situation in the family." The situation of women in the family, in turn, "varies with the nature of the family": "According to the manner in which the family is composed and organized, the woman plays a role which is more or less important" (1980, 274). More intangible than legal status is something Durkheim calls the "moral importance" or "moral equality" of women. The moral importance of women's role in the family is contingent on the social significance and internal vitality of the family. Historically, the moral importance of the woman's or "wife's" role increased where "domestic life had a greater place in the context of life in general" and where "the conjugal association became more strongly organized" (1980, 209).

Conversely, a "loose conjugal relationship" is associated with "the independence of the wife vis-à-vis the husband." This relative independence has the effect of rendering the spouses "strangers" to each other, a condition that constitutes "the greatest obstacle in bringing about moral equality between the two sexes" (1980, 303).

Women should seek equality in functions commensurate with their nature, in natural, biological, affective functions—in domestic bliss. They should seek status through the status of the family in the eyes of society, in the eyes of men. Therefore, paradoxically, the interests of women are aligned with the interests of the traditional family. To strengthen the traditional family, both externally in terms of absolute social sanctity and internally in terms of absolute intimate unity, is to strengthen the position of women, situated rightfully and absolutely within it. The ideal structure of the family, reflecting the joint, identical interests of females and families, is actually patriarchy.

Sources of Family Strength: Integration and Regulation

Women desiring equality must do two things, according to Durkheim. They must specialize in the family, and they must strengthen the family. He views domestic specialization as natural and unproblematic for women and therefore does no more than recommend it. But with respect to enhancing the position of women by reinforcing the female, familial institution, he actively proposes some concrete measures. The nature of these measures is suggested by the nature of the family as Durkheim conceives it. For Durkheim the family is a society. Therefore, logically, the strength of domestic society has the same two dimensions as the strength of any society: integration and regulation. A strong family is a solidary family, and a solidary family comprises integrated and regulated individuals. The family is successfully integrated in two related ways: through the sexual division of labor and through the sexual stratification of authority.

FAMILY INTEGRATION THROUGH SEXUAL SPECIALIZATION

In the first place, the individual members of a family are integrated through the sexual division of labor. The sexual division of labor creates organic solidarity in conjugal society. In fact, it actually constitutes conjugal society. The more women and men are differentiated and specialized—the more they are different from each other in structure and function—the greater their interdependence, and the stronger their marital and familial unity. Thus if women want equality with men, they must be different from men: the more they are different, the more they are equal, because difference solidifies the domestic society to which women are consigned by nature.

Durkheim "describes" the causal "fact" that "the sexual division of labor is the source of conjugal solidarity" and the historical "fact" that the sexual division of labor "has developed concomitant with conjugal solidarity" (1933, 56). Conversely, he "describes" the reverse—the negation of sexual/marital/familial relations, society, solidarity. "The state of marriage in societies where the two sexes are only weakly differentiated thus evinces conjugal solidarity which is itself very weak. Permit the sexual division of labor to recede below a certain level and conjugal society would eventually subsist in sexual relations preeminently ephemeral" (59, 61).

Durkheim's description of the sexual division of labor constitutes more an implicit endorsement of it than an overt exhortation to sexual specialization. It is more an apologia, an enumeration of the positive features, the necessary and beneficial functions, of an extant, ineluctable social fact. There is no need to advocate the necessary, the natural, the inevitable. There is only a need to circumvent attempted alterations of it; in other words, to demonstrate its necessity and naturalness and inevitability. The demonstration of necessity serves, implicitly, as a demonstration of the futility of effecting effective change. And since the necessary is also the beneficial, what is inescapable for people is also good for them. Therefore Durkheim, in describing the *functions* of the sexual division of labor, is reconciling men and women to their fate and simultaneously reconciling them to their fortune. In describing/defending the sexual division of labor, Durkheim is not so much prescribing social action as implying that social action is contraindicated.

There is just one moment when Durkheim feels compelled to call into question the sexual division of labor, to suggest that it is arbitrary rather than automatic, a happy but not totally predetermined outcome. In *The Division of Labor,* he points out the existence of alternative familial types and alternative sexual relations. He is forced to admit that, although "circumstances" tend to cause sexual specialization, nevertheless "they are not sufficient to determine the specialization." The "circumstances" that are necessary but insufficient causes of the sexual division of labor consist in the "differences" between men and women. Sexual differences "make possible the division of labor" but "do not necessitate it." If specialization occurs, it occurs in accordance with these "natural differences"; it respects and reflects them. If men and women specialize, they perform the functions that coincide with their specific natures. Yet this apparently natural arrangement is not necessarily a necessary arrangement (1933, 264–65).

Of course, when Durkheim discusses alternative sexual/familial relationships, he is referring to ancient societies and families. But his underlying concern is undoubtedly with the future. He is afraid that feminists, seeking sexual equality, will seek to reestablish sexual similarity, that they will not be dissuaded by its characterization as "primitive." Therefore Durkheim goes further and characterizes sexual equality as inimical to the interests of women. Sexual equality, as sexual similarity, engenders mechanical, ephemeral, sexual/familial solidarity. Since the status of women depends on the strength of the family, women have no choice but to seek organic familial solidarity, and therefore they have no choice but to seek exaggerated sexual specialization. Durkheim defends the sexual division of labor as directly functional for the family—and therefore as indirectly functional for women. He promotes the sexual division of labor as familialist and therefore as feminist.

FAMILY INTEGRATION THROUGH SEXUAL STRATIFICATION

According to Durkheim, the second way the family—women's bastion—can be integrated and fortified is through a specific, vertical dimension of the sexual division of labor: the institution of sexual stratification. The hierarchical aspect of the sexual division of labor appears exclusively as male authority. Males are structurally suited to functionally specialize in the exercise of power; females are naturally predisposed to specialize in the practice of subordination. Like the entire sexual division of labor, male authority is natural and functional, and therefore probable. But like the entire sexual division of labor, male authority is not completely inevitable and ubiquitous. Durkheim declares that "Because of *age,* because of the *blood relations* he has with his children, the father *is* the one who exercises the authority in the family, an authority constituting paternal power" (1933, 265; emphasis added). He contrasts this finding with its empirical negation: "*Nevertheless,* in the matriarchal family, it is not in him that this authority rests" (1933, 265; emphasis added).

Like the alternative to the sexual division of labor, sexual homogeneity, Durkheim views the egalitarian alternative to patriarchy as a thing of the past, part of an obsolete society. Nonetheless, just as he fears a regression to sexual similarity, he fears the reincarnation of sexual parity as feminists atavistically protest against patriarchy. Durkheim cannot rely, therefore, solely on a defense of patriarchy as an extant and modern—and therefore functional and evolved— structure. He cannot rely solely on a denunciation of nonpatriarchal sexual politics as primitive. Feminists, with their overriding objective of equality, could seek to surpass the present and return to the prepatriarchal past. Durkheim must find a way to defend patriarchy as feminist.

First he defends patriarchy against the charge that it constitutes an "enslavement of women," calling such a proposition "most disputable." He asserts that it is possible to "unjustly" downgrade Roman patriarchy and that attacks, like defenses, are ultimately in vain. The patriarchal system can be judged only against its social context, which produces and "justifies" it. For Durkheim the relationship of male "supremacy" and "protection" and female "submission" and "self-sacrifice" constitutes a "subordination" that is in no way "degrading." Durkheim's first defense of patriarchy is defensive: patriarchy is not anti-feminist.

His main line of defense is positive, though. Patriarchy actually advances the interests of women because it advances the interests of the family. One source of "feminine grandeur" is family strength. One source of family strength is familial integration. And the paramount form of familial integration is patriarchy. Patriarchy creates a strong and holy family and thereby engenders reverence for the women of the family.[3]

The patriarchal family is the modern family. It supplants the primitive communistic clan, which is essentially amorphous: extended and homogeneous, simple and mechanically integrated. By contrast, the patriarchal family is organized and delimited. It manifests the universal law of all natural evolution, the law of differentiation and specialization. And it manifests the universal law of all familial evolution, the "law of contraction or progressive emergence" (1965a, 536). But the patriarchal family evolves still further, into the "conjugal family." And patriarchal authority evolves into "conjugal authority."

Conjugal authority, like patriarchy, is necessary. It is the natural form of organization of the highest family type. More important, conjugal authority, like patriarchy, is beneficial. The subordination of the wife under the husband's power is "needed" for "good conjugal discipline" and "the shared interest of the household" (1980, 218). The most crucial function of conjugal authority, however, is that it creates strong marital and family unity in the same way that patriarchy does. The male authority/female subordination relation is ultimately "*a means of unifying the conjugal society*" (1980, 260; emphasis added): "It is inevitable that, at least at a given moment in history, the matrimonial bond cannot become tightly constricting and the family cannot hold together without a resulting legal subordination of the wife to her husband." In fact, "*this subordination is the necessary condition of family unity*" (1980, 209; emphasis added).

Male supremacy in the nuclear family is thus posed as feminist in two senses. First, male conjugal authority is feminist because it is *like* patriarchy. Like patriarchy, in unifying domestic society it renders the family more potent and thereby enhances the position of women, the family functionaries. Second, male conjugal authority is feminist because it is *unlike* patriarchy. Male conjugal authority is even more feminist than patriarchy because it renders the male as husband less potent than the male as father.

Although conjugal authority is essentially a contracted and "tempered" version of patriarchal authority, it can still be excessive. Excessive conjugal authority reflects a vestigial survival of the patriarchal form of the family. It results from the maintenance of the transitional Roman power structure in the advanced European family. The "supremacy of the husband" and the "subordination of the wife" are problematic only in degree, not in nature, in quantity rather than in quality; and then primarily with respect to the joint conjugal property arrangement: they constitute "vexations that tie up property settlements and paralyze other transactions."

It is Durkheim's practical recommendation, then, that the modern, conjugal form of familial authority should not be *modified* but should be *moderated* still further so that it is, like all natural, normal, and functional things, moderate rather than excessive. Abnormal levels of male supremacy and female subordination "are due to an unwarranted conception of marital prerogatives." Therefore Durkheim concludes that "the only way to remedy them is to renounce such a conception, to make the ordinary wife the equal of the husband, to increase her powers and her participation in the administration of the matters at hand" (1980, 294).

A preferable family power relationship exists in the European family, which is free from Roman influence. In the European family the husband is "placed in charge" while the wife is "put . . . in a subordinate position in relation to him." This system not only is necessary, as "indispensable to domestic discipline." It is also beneficial to women. The European wife is not subject to legal subordination as incapable. She is "simply" "subject to her husband in the running of the family" (1980, 260–61).

After defending patriarchy, Durkheim acknowledges the feminist position by situating patriarchy in a historical context, by claiming that it is in fact outmoded, replaced by a more limited, conjugal authority appropriate to the new conjugal family. After defending conjugal authority as functional—as necessary, or inevitable, and as beneficial, or desirable—Durkheim acknowledges the feminist position by acknowledging excesses of conjugal authority, attributing them to the anachronistic persistence of patriarchy, and advocating amelioration without structural change.

Durkheim's encounter with feminism leads him back to the Roman patriarchal family. Roman patriarchy is, remarkably, presented as a feminist ideal. The patriarchal system constitutes the strongest form of the family and therefore, ironically, the most advantageous situation for women. The "family," "marital," or "conjugal" power structure that succeeds patriarchy is nothing more than a refinement of it. Women achieve fulfillment in the family and therefore are situated there. Once women are situated in and identified with the family, they achieve status to the extent that the family derives strength and salience. This strength and salience, in turn, derive from the integrating influences of sexual specialization and sexual stratification.

Conversely, the "equalization of wife and husband" is a condition that "can compromise the organic unity of conjugal society and of the family" (1978c, 143). Women seeking equality must do so by taking their place in a strong family. A strong family is contingent on sexual difference and inequality. To be equal, women must be different from men and subordinate to them.

FAMILY STRENGTH THROUGH SEXUAL REGULATION

The sexual division of labor and male authority strengthen the family through integration. Like any other society, however, the family is a group of individuals that is consolidated through regulation as well as integration. Like any other society, the family counters the centrifugal egocentricity of individuals by linking them to one another and to the collective. Like any other society, it counters the anarchic avidity of individuals by restraining their desires and orchestrating their movements. The viability or solidarity of any society, including the family, is contingent on two things: the ascendance of collective integration over individual alienation, and the ascendance of collective regulation over individual anomie.

Most commonly, anomie is understood as general social lawlessness. Durkheim describes it as a temporary lack of rules for behavior and interaction, characteristic of emergent social elements. Alternatively, anomie is described as a lack of limits on individual aspirations, which Durkheim conceptualizes primarily in economic terms. Economic anomie represents the unfettered and therefore infinite and insatiable pecuniary desires of individuals set free from the rigid and well-defined constraints of the feudal system. But Durkheim also discusses yet another form of anomie; another materialistic perversion, another pathological passion for the infinite unleashed in modern society. And that is sexual anomie.

Sexual anomie is the problem, and marriage is the solution. For Durkheim the primary function of marriage, superseding its integrative function, is the regulation of sexual desire. A factor that contributes to the solution of the problem, to sexual regulation, is the indissolubility of marriage. Marriage constitutes, essentially and above all, a "regulation of sexual relations." Its main necessary and beneficial effect is that it "completely regulates the life of passion." It accomplishes this because, and to the extent that, it "assigns a strictly definite object to the need for love, and closes the horizon" (1951, 270).

A factor that contributes to the problem, to sexual anomie, is the availability of divorce. Divorce by mutual consent, along with sexual equality, tends to "compromise the organic unity of conjugal society" (1978c, 143). Divorce irreversibly shatters the monogamous ordering of sex, which is the very essence of marriage. Marital sexual monogamy is posed as an absolute, and divorce is posed as its absolute negation: the possibility of divorce represents the possibility of infinite sexual relations. Therefore, in the presence of divorce, a "morbid desire for the infinite" emerges within sexuality (1951, 271). When sexual appetites are not totally limited, they become totally unlimited. Divorce introduces anarchy into sexuality, thereby destroying domestic society and nullifying its main function.

The first casualty of this inherently asocial condition is marriage itself. Divorce has "a very dangerous influence on marriage and its normal functioning"

(1978a, 240–41). It prevents marriage from "playing its role" as a force of restraint and moderation and thus eliminates its "principal reason for existing" (1978a, 248). Divorce engenders "a weakening of matrimonial regulation." Where divorce exists, "marriage is nothing but a weakened simulacrum of itself" (1951, 271). In fact, where divorce by mutual consent is allowed, marriage actually "ceases to be itself": "Regulation from which one can withdraw whenever one has a notion is no longer regulation. A restraint from which one can so easily liberate oneself is no longer a restraint which can moderate desires and, in moderating them, appease them" (1978a, 248).

65 ·

Durkheim's theory is that marriage creates sexual regulation whereas divorce, by destroying marriage, creates sexual anomie. The empirical evidence for this theory consists of suicide statistics. Durkheim demonstrates that indissoluble marriage is associated with lower suicide rates, while legalized divorce is associated with higher suicide rates. His explanation for these dramatic results is that marriage, by providing sexual regulation, prevents sexual anomie and therefore prevents anomic suicide. Conversely divorce, by disrupting sexual regulation, causes sexual anomie and therefore causes anomic suicide.

The problem Durkheim encounters is that this pattern is true only of men. The suicide rates of women indicate an entirely different—in fact, an opposite—pattern. Among women indissoluble marriage is associated with increased suicide rates, while divorce by mutual consent is associated with decreased suicide rates. Durkheim concludes that the interests of men and women are not unitary but opposed, particularly with respect to marriage. There is an "antagonism of the sexes" that "prevents marriage favoring them equally" (1951, 274). Within the family, as marital partners, the interests of men and women "are different and often hostile" (269). The interests of husband and wife in marriage are "obviously opposed" (384). Specifically, marriage is relatively beneficial for men, relatively detrimental for women: "In general the wife profits less from family life than the husband . . . in itself conjugal society is harmful to the woman and aggravates her tendency to suicide" (188–89).

Durkheim ignores the critical, even radical, implications of these findings. In fact he first constructs a conservative scientific explanation and then formulates a reactionary policy recommendation. Durkheim explains the differential effects of marriage and divorce in terms of the differential natures of men and women. The "antagonism" between the sexes is caused by the fact that "the two sexes do not share equally in social life" (1951, 385). Men, as social beings, have socially created, mental desires that are potentially infinite. Therefore they need social regulation, socially imposed restraints that limit their desires, to achieve moderation and satiation. Women, as asocial creatures, have only naturally created, physical drives. Therefore they are subject to natural regulation and naturally imposed restraints: their drives are spontaneously limited and finite. Women are simultaneously driven and governed by instincts: instincts are compelling, but they are inherently moderate and satiable.[4]

Given his own discovery, the conflict of interest dividing men and women over marriage and divorce, Durkheim is forced to make a choice. In recommending policy to combat the social problems of which suicide is symptomatic, he must choose between pro-marriage measures, which would reduce anomie and male suicide rates, and pro-divorce measures, which would reduce fatalism and female suicide rates. He recognizes the problem, but it gives him little cause for hesitation. Durkheim decides to support indissoluble marriage and the interests of men. He decides to attack divorce, anomie, anomic suicide, male suicide—and the interests of women. "The only way to reduce the number of suicides due to conjugal anomy is to make marriage indissoluble." Unfortunately, "the suicides of husbands cannot be diminished in this way without increasing those of wives": "*Must one of the sexes necessarily be sacrificed, and is the solution only to choose the lesser of two evils? Nothing else seems possible*" (1951, 384; emphasis added).

Durkheim uncovers some potentially feminist social facts: the interests of men and women are opposed; marriage is beneficial to men at the expense of women; divorce is beneficial to women at the expense of men. He recuperates his own radical discovery immediately, in *Suicide,* with a decidedly nonfeminist interpretation and a decidedly nonfeminist policy position. He is not content with this solution, however, and eventually writes an article retracting his own original findings.[5]

In "Divorce by Mutual Consent," Durkheim replaces his theory that divorce has a positive effect on women with the theory that divorce has *no effect* on women. "It does not seem that the practice of divorce affects feminine suicide in an appreciable way" (1978a, 246). Similarly, he replaces his theory that marriage has a negative effect on women with the theory that marriage has *no effect* on women. There is a "general law" according to which "the state of marriage has only a weak effect on the moral constitution of women" (247). Remarkably, his explanation for these new conclusions is the same as his explanation for the old conclusions. Divorce and marriage have no effect on women because women are fundamentally asocial.

Durkheim arbitrarily eliminates the opposition between men and women that he had inadvertently exposed in *Suicide.* He recants those of his theories that implicitly bolster feminist criticisms of marriage and feminist arguments for divorce. In "Divorce by Mutual Consent" he sets up a new opposition. He replaces the conflict between men and women over marriage and divorce with a conflict between society and the individual. Divorce, Durkheim asserts, is a measure that ostensibly favors individuals, but at the expense of the institution of marriage and of society itself. Divorce might be in the individual interest, but indissoluble marriage is in the social interest, and the social interest always takes precedence.

Marriage serves society, and divorce hinders marriage. Therefore, regardless of its value to individuals, divorce cannot be tolerated. Individual evils are inherently less grave than social maladies. But remedying individual evils is only a "pretext" for legalizing divorce. Durkheim contends that the pretext is false: divorce not only harms society, it also fails to help individuals. In fact, according to Durkheim, divorce actually harms individuals. Individuals have only an apparent interest in divorce; individual and social interests are only apparently opposed. In reality, there is a congruence of interest uniting society and the individual: both benefit from the institution of marriage and suffer from the introduction of divorce.

Marriage is directly necessary and beneficial for individuals. Marriage regulates individuals, makes them satiable and happy, and prevents anomic suicide. By limiting their desires, it provides satisfaction. Marriage has a "moderating and salutary effect," which is "its principal reason for existing" (1978a, 248). Marriage exerts a "moral influence," which "*benefits the individuals themselves*": "*Man can be happy and can satisfy his desires in a normal way only if he is regulated, contained, moderated and disciplined*" (247, 252; emphasis added).

Conversely, divorce is directly deleterious to individuals. It deregulates them, makes them insatiable and unhappy, and increases their tendency to commit suicide. Divorce causes individual misery: the sexual passion for the infinite that it unleashes is essentially a "painful condition." Deregulation is primarily a social problem, but it is an acute individual problem as well. "*Conjugal discipline cannot be weakened without also affecting the happiness of the spouses. . . . The individuals themselves would be the first to suffer for it*" (1978a, 252; emphasis added). Divorce "destroys" marriage; the destruction of marriage in turn constitutes "a grave social malady"; and finally, this grave social malady has "repercussions" that "the individual would bear" (240–41).

Durkheim's argument against divorce is in effect overdetermined. First he describes the interests of men and women as opposed and takes the side of men. Divorce should be prohibited to prevent male anomie and suicide, despite an increase in female fatalism and suicide. He then repudiates his own analysis and claims that divorce has no effect on women and that therefore, with respect to divorce, women are disinterested. He declares that the interests of men and women are identical because women have no interests. Divorce should be prohibited to benefit men, at no cost to women.

Next Durkheim suggests that it is the interests of society and individuals that are opposed and takes the side of society. Divorce ameliorates individual conditions but damages the institution of marriage and therefore damages society. Divorce should be prohibited as destructive of an institutional element of the social fabric: familial solidarity, integration, and especially regulation. The interests of marriage, the family, and society take precedence over individual interests if there is a conflict.

However, Durkheim goes on to suggest that, like the male/female conflict of interest, the societal/individual conflict of interest is more apparent than real. Just as he ends by aligning the interests of women with the interests of men, so he ends by aligning the interests of individuals with those of society and its institutions. Despite the perception that divorce is beneficial for individuals, it is in reality injurious to them both directly, through anomie and suicide, and indirectly, through the damage individuals incur when the social organism and its organs are damaged. Divorce should be prohibited to prevent anomie and suicide, as well as institutional and social breakdown, because these phenomena directly and indirectly harm the individual cells of society.[6]

Finally, in the ultimate moment of overdetermination, Durkheim opposes divorce from a feminist standpoint. Whether he acknowledges that legal divorce spares women fatalism and suicide, as in *Suicide,* or suggests that it has no appreciable effect on women, as in "Divorce by Mutual Consent," he views divorce as inimical to the objective interests of women. This is because, as indicated above, he believes that the true interests of women are advanced by bolstering the family. Women's place is in the home, and therefore the home must be reinforced, fortified, and elevated to consolidate and sanctify women's position and thereby women. Divorce has the opposite effect: it destroys women's domestic sanctuary, marriage and family, and thereby disintegrates and devalues women's social position and thus women themselves. One way or another, one way *and* another, Durkheim establishes a harmony of interests, linking women's best interests, their genuine welfare, with the welfare of men, the patriarchal family, and society itself.

The Appropriation of Feminism: Equal but Different

Durkheim does not explicitly present his antidivorce position as "feminist." The connection between the prohibition of divorce and his conception of the underlying, authentic interests of women is indirect and implicit. It must be teased out from Durkheim's theoretical framework, taking into account his particular view of feminism and his belief in the pro-female ramifications of pro-family policy. His explicit "feminist" formulations are as follows: (1) Women should seek equality through the realization of their own singular nature. (2) Women's generic nature predisposes them in particular to the affective functions found in the family. (3) Since the welfare and identity of women are naturally and inextricably linked to those of the family, the collective condition and position of women can be enhanced by strengthening the distaff, domestic domain. This set of propositions culminates logically, but implicitly, in the equation of women's interests with pro-family measures: the integrative measures of sexual specialization and conjugal authority and the regulative measure of indissoluble monogamous marriage.

Durkheim makes one explicit concession to feminism that lies outside this scheme. He writes one prescription for women that places them outside the home. Durkheim admits the possibility of "feminine" functions in the public or social sphere. In fact, he endorses female participation in the public sphere as long as it is confined to feminine functions. His initial motivation is to resolve the difference of interest apparently dividing women and men, as revealed in the suicide data. Specifically, he wishes to rectify the situation in which marriage can be said to "favor" one sex "to the detriment of the other."

Marriage, Durkheim says, "cannot simultaneously be agreeable to two persons, one of whom is almost entirely the product of society, while the other has remained to a far greater extent the product of nature." There is an antagonism between men and women, "the interests of husband and wife in marriage are so obviously opposed," primarily because "the two sexes do not share equally in social life." Durkheim's initial solution to this problem, in *Suicide,* is to adopt a partisan position and support marriage in "favor" of men and "to the detriment" of women. Conversely, he opposes divorce to preserve marriage and men, despite the attendant "lesser" evil, the "sacrifice" of women to fatalistic suicide. His ultimate solution, in "Divorce by Mutual Consent," is to deny that a sex-based conflict of interest over marriage and divorce exists. He advocates indissoluble marriage as good for men with no effect on women. He opposes divorce by mutual consent as bad for men with no effect on women. Yet Durkheim also poses a third, intermediate, solution. He suggests fleetingly that certain differences in the respective conditions of women and men could be reduced in order to reduce the difference of interest between them.

In *Suicide,* just after pronouncing the notorious "lesser of two evils" decision, Durkheim devises an auxiliary approach to the sexually divided divorce dilemma. There is a "remedy" to the antagonism between the sexes, the antagonism arising out of the fact that man is social and woman is natural. In another variation on the different but equal theme, men and women can become "socially equalized." This will occur as women are increasingly "able to play a part in society." The "social" equality of the sexes, achieved through female activity outside the family, in "society" itself, has Durkheim's approval—with one absolute and inviolable condition. Women's role in society can conceivably be "more active and important than that of today." But it must necessarily be *"peculiarly her own."* Men and women may be "socially equalized, *but in different ways."*

Durkheim is not suggesting that women become similar to men in structure or function. In fact, his recommendation that they enter the social world is embedded in a passage rife with injunctions to the contrary. The opposition between natural woman and social man will not diminish. In fact, "it was originally less marked than now." Durkheim notes that "evolution" is widening the gap between the sexes, as evidenced by the fact that "woman differs from man much more in cities than in the country": "To be sure, we have no reason to suppose that woman may ever be able to fulfill the same functions in society as man. . . . The female sex will not again become more similar to the male; on the contrary, we may foresee that it will become more different" (1951, 385). There is a "flagrant psychological inequality" between the sexes, which represents "the work of centuries," which cannot be instantly abolished, and which renders equal rights or "juridical equality" illegitimate. The sexual difference cannot be denied or altered. It is both eternal and evolutionary. On the other hand, it can be put to good use. Durkheim predicts that while the female sex will become more different from the male, "these differences will become of greater social use than in the past." Specifically, women can assume some of the public but superfluous functions so that men may become increasingly specialized in strictly useful and significant work.

"Why," Durkheim asks, "should not aesthetic functions become woman's?" Aesthetic functions, presumably, are not at odds with women's "affective" nature. Furthermore, in modern productive, industrial society, men no longer have time for the frivolous and the nonproductive—in other words, for aesthetic activities. The aesthetic functions become woman's "as man, more and more absorbed by functions of utility, has to renounce them" (1951, 385).

In pursuing the "artistic and literary life," women realize their feminine essence: "Even in this sphere of action, woman carries out her own nature, and her role is very specialized, very different from that of man" (1933, 60). The entrance of women into the public sphere, within the artistic domain, expresses and enhances the sexual division of labor rather than reversing it: "This apparent return to primitive homogeneity is nothing else than the beginning of a new differentiation." What is more, this new differentiation frees men from a relatively affective function, art, for a more purely intellectual function, science. "Further, if arts and letters begin to become feminine tasks, the other sex seems to permit it in order to give itself more specially to the pursuit of science" (60). Durkheim makes a feminist concession, allowing that women can and even should realize their own natures and attain "social" equality by emigrating out of the family and immigrating into public life. Women's unique nature predisposes them to "affective" functions—meaning, almost exclusively, family functions. But the "almost," the exception to domesticity constituted by the aesthetic realm, is a crucial exception. It allows women to "come out," to debut in society, to play a public role. However, Durkheim seems to have other than feminist motivations for this surprise move. He seems to have a nonfeminist agenda, which he portrays in a feminist light, as part of his compromise with/of feminism.

In advocating the partial and restricted integration of women into public and social life, the betterment of women's lives is not Durkheim's objective. His actual objectives are threefold: (1) To reduce the contrast between men and women, thereby rendering the effects of marriage more uniform and vitiating feminist criticism of marriage as well as feminist support for divorce. (2) To further differentiate the functions of the sexes, isolating the affective functions from the intellectual functions even in public life. (3) To free men from "feminine" (read "effeminate") or "aesthetic" (read "useless") occupations, so they can concentrate their efforts on masculine, intellectual "functions of utility" and science. Durkheim advocates the feminization of the arts not for reasons of feminism but for reasons of social utility—for the "greater social use" that can be gained from intensifying sexual heterogeneity and extending the sexual division of labor into the public world.

The description of women's new, public but aesthetic, place is equivocal in several senses. First, under the guise of "equalizing" the sexes, it does so strictly "in different ways." "Both sexes would thus approximate each other by their very differences" (1951, 385). From ghettoization in the devalued domestic sphere, or private life, women can move to ghettoization in the devalued aesthetic sphere of public life. Their different and inferior station in life is not to be transcended, but will merely be transposed into a new setting. Further, the true motivation behind the move is not the welfare and liberation of women, but rather the welfare of society and the liberation of men.

Durkheim's gesture toward women is in essence duplicitous. In addition, even this hypocritical, pseudofeminist "concession" is perhaps negated by the article "Divorce by Mutual Consent." In *The Division of Labor* Durkheim merely describes the feminization of arts and letters as a continuation rather than a reversal of evolutionary sexual differentiation. In *Suicide* he actually advocates relegating women to aesthetics and aesthetics to women as a palliative for the battle of the sexes over marriage and divorce. However, in "Divorce by Mutual Consent" he eliminates the problem—the sexual difference of interest— and thereby removes the ulterior motive behind the solution, the specialization of the *beau sexe* in the beaux arts and belles lettres.

Durkheim makes one final extrafamilial feminist proposal. It is as ambiguous and ambivalent as the first, the aesthetic option for women. Durkheim takes a liberal stance, usually reserved for men, on the issue of female occupational specialization. He argues that the sexual division of labor need not be a matter of law. Sex roles need not be legally codified and mandated. Women, like serfs, could be legally emancipated from ascribed statuses, from a hereditary system of prescribed and proscribed labor. The sexual caste system, like the feudal caste system, could be overturned. In a footnote, he describes the extension of individual mobility to women, with tacit approval: "It may be foreseen that this differentiation would probably no longer have the strictly regulative character that it has today. Woman would not be officially excluded from certain functions and relegated to others. She could choose more freely" (1951, 385).

The apparent contradiction between this statement and Durkheim's vehement defense of a rigid sexual division of labor is instantly resolved. In the same breath Durkheim undercuts the liberal feminist import of this vision and belies his true conservatism and sexism.[7] It is acceptable to create de jure equal opportunity for women, to allow them to "choose more freely": it is acceptable because it is safe. Legal freedom of employment is in Durkheim's view a feminist concession that incurs no cost or disruption to the extant sexual system. Individual occupational mobility is permissible for women because it is—for women—ultimately meaningless. The social, artificial measure is nullified by a more powerful force: nature.

Equal opportunity under the law is perfectly harmless because it is perfectly ineffectual. It cannot overwrite the essence of the sexes, the difference and inequality that define them and that are inscribed by nature itself. Therefore it cannot modify the social arrangements that express and reflect this natural, essential, immutable difference and inequality. Sexual specialization, segregation, and stratification are natural social facts: they are social facts that are caused by natural facts and as such they cannot be undone. The social has force only to the extent that it is grounded in the natural. Therefore Durkheim can cavalierly imagine "woman" being able, according to juridical law, to "choose more freely." This is because he has faith in a higher, more imperative law—the law of nature.

She could choose more freely, "*but as her choice would be determined by her aptitudes, it would generally bear on the same sort of occupations. It would be perceptibly uniform, though not obligatory*" (1951, 385; emphasis added).

The sexual division of labor does not have to be legally "obligatory," because it is naturally obligatory. Occupations do not need to be determined by human law, because they are "determined" by natural law. The law of nature determines, definitively, the nature of woman, her natural "aptitudes." The nature of woman determines, definitively, the nature of woman's work—like her, naturally "uniform." Elsewhere Durkheim denounces juridical equality as unnatural and illegitimate: "Juridical equality cannot be legitimate so long as psychological inequality is so flagrant." Here he dismisses juridical equality as unviable and innocuous. Durkheim does not fear formal sexual equality because he believes that ultimately no human tribunal can join what natural decree has put asunder: Man and Woman, Man's Work and Woman's Work.

Chapter **4**

CONTRADICTIONS:

THE

PROBLEM OF

WOMEN

▪ Durkheim's oeuvre is rife with contradictions. Because of the immensity and intricacy of his theory, of the social universe and historical juncture he theorizes, and of the extratheoretical factors impinging on his theoretical processes, the self-contradictory nature of Durkheim's theoretical edifice is in a sense inevitable.

The tendency of Durkheim's theory is to complexity, to conflicting tendencies. Yet there are some regions where his thought is quite coherent, or at least where coherence can be convincingly reconstructed. In these regions Durkheim either has only one consistent position or he has a predominant position that can be discerned despite real or apparent pretenders. This chapter is concerned with three such regions, or positions, within Durkheim's work. It examines the way Durkheim's thinking makes sense, and the way it makes sense of three separate theoretical problems.

Primarily, however, it looks at how this sense is rendered nonsensical, this order is rendered chaotic, and this coherence is rendered incoherent by the introduction of a new problem. Specifically, this chapter addresses the way certain central dimensions of Durkheim's sociological theory are disrupted when he theorizes about women.[1] This disruption itself, in fact, constitutes another area of congruity in Durkheim's work. His formulations about women tend, uniformly, to disturb and belie—to contradict—theoretical patterns that otherwise prevail.

The Theory of Organicism

Durkheim's organicism structures his entire theoretical system. The core, governing tenets are very simple. Society resembles a biological organism: its institutions and occupations resemble biological organs, and its individual members resemble biological cells. According to some interpretations this organic theory of society is metaphorical: Durkheim's organicism consists of an elaborate organic analogy. According to others Durkheim's organicism is quite literal: the social organism, with its collective body and mind, is an actual, ultracomplex entity composed of individual human organisms.

Whether literal or metaphorical, organicism is the dominant theoretical principle in Durkheim's work. As such it has infinite logical implications, many of which Durkheim elaborates, in all their complexity, with flawless consistency. One such implication concerns the relationship among the individual members or elements or cells of the social organism. The principle of organicism implies the organic *unity* of all individuals who compose society.

The fundamental relationship of unity in society is determined by a fundamental relationship of functionality. Every part in society is functional for every other part, and for society as a whole. The whole society in turn is functional for every social element. Individuals function like cells in relation to other cells, organs, and the organism. They perform necessary and beneficial functions for other individuals, for institutions (including specialized industries and occupations), and for the emergent society. Institutions function like organs in relation to other organs, cells, and the organism. They perform necessary and beneficial functions for other institutions, for individuals, and for the emergent society. Finally, the emergent society functions like an organism in relation to its organs and cells. It performs necessary and beneficial functions for its constituent institutions and individuals.

The necessary and beneficial functions linking parts with parts and parts with the whole, in society as in an organism, create bonds of interrelationship and interdependence. Furthermore, the organic principle implies a single common interest that links the interests of all elemental parts of an organism or a society. That single common interest is the health and welfare of the organism itself, on which the health and welfare of its components absolutely depend.

Finally, the functional unity that organizes society implies that all the individual elements of society benefit equally from the health, welfare, and normal functioning of social institutions and the social whole. This is the case, just as all of the cells in an organism derive undifferentiated benefits from the health, welfare and normal functioning of organs and the organism. No cell/individual needs the biological/social organs and organism more or less than any other; none benefits more or less than any other. The common interest that integrates individuals is not only common, but equally shared. Thus the unity of individuals, like the unity of cells, is perfect.

It is this precept of organicism, the precept of organic unity, that Durkheim violates in his discussion of men, women, marriage, and divorce (1951). This is the only instance in Durkheim's work where he conceptualizes a systematic division among individuals: a division of individuals into distinct and antagonistic groups. This is the only situation where Durkheim theorizes a conflict of interest, bisecting society into two opposing factions. His thesis about men, women, marriage, and divorce is suggested not deductively, by the organic social theory it totally contradicts, but inductively, by his suicide statistics.

Durkheim's suicide statistics suggest that the social institution of marriage has a differential, diametric effect on women as opposed to men. Likewise divorce, the negation of marriage, has one effect on men; another, contrary effect on women. Thus, with respect to marriage and divorce, there are irreconcilable differences which separate the interests of men and women.

Specifically, married men commit suicide less frequently than non-married men. Conversely, married women commit suicide more frequently than non-married women.[2] Second, in regions where divorce exists, men commit suicide more frequently than where it is prohibited. Conversely, where divorce exists, women commit suicide less frequently than where it is prohibited.

Durkheim explains these findings as demonstrating that marriage has a positive effect on men and a negative effect on women, while divorce has a negative effect on men and a positive effect on women. He explains these effects as mediated by sexual regulation and sexual anomie. Men need the sexual regulation of marriage and suffer from the sexual anomie of the unmarried state or the accessibility of divorce.[3] Women's sexuality is physiologically regulated; therefore marriage is neither necessary nor beneficial but is an unmitigated constraint.[4] Divorce provides at most escape from marriage and at least the possibility of escape, which renders marriage more tolerable.[5]

Durkheim is unequivocal in his description of the hostile interests and positions of men and women. There is an "antagonism" between the sexes based on their natural differences. The antagonism originates "because the two sexes do not share equally in social life" (1951, 385). Because men are naturally social and women are naturally natural, they have different needs and different relationships to society and social institutions. An institution "cannot simultaneously be agreeable to two persons, one of whom is almost entirely the product of society, while the other has remained to a far greater extent the product of nature" (385). Specifically, the "antagonism of the sexes . . . prevents marriage favoring them equally . . . their interests are contrary; one needs restraint and the other liberty" (274). The interests of men and women can be reconciled in their roles as parents, where "they have the same object." But as men and women and in relation to marriage—as "partners"—"their interests are different and often hostile" (269).

Since Durkheim attributes the conflict between women and men to the differences that separate them, he sees no resolution apart from a convergence of the sexes. "Only when the difference between husband and wife becomes less, will marriage no longer be thought, so to speak, necessarily to favor one to the detriment of the other" (1951, 386). Durkheim, however, proposes measures to alleviate the tension between the sexes that would maintain or even exacerbate sexual differences. Specifically, he recommends that women should become more social and enter into public life, though only in decidedly "feminine" roles.[6]

Presumably Durkheim envisions that public life would socialize women's sexuality so that eventually they, like men, would benefit from the sexual regulation of indissoluble marriage and suffer from the sexual anomie of legal divorce. He loses track of the original intent of his proposal, however, and focuses instead on the positive effects of this new sexual division of labor on men and on society.[7] Furthermore, there are inherent limits to this sexual similarity through dissimilarity, this modern primitivism, this resemblance through difference.

In the first place, there is already a deep, irreconcilable schism between men and women. Men and women are radically separated by a "flagrant" structural difference or "psychological inequality" (1951, 386). This schism or inequality consists precisely in the gap between the intrinsically social nature of men and the intrinsically asocial nature of women. In the second place, the sexes are becoming increasingly differentiated, as part of the inexorable, universal, natural process of evolution. "The female sex will not again become more similar to the male; on the contrary, we may foresee that it will become more different"

(385). Third, sexual specialization in general, and the patriarchal family in particular, is "functional."

The convergence through divergence of the two sexes is a dubious and long-term—if not impossible and undesirable—solution to the problem of the sexual conflict of interest. Durkheim also proposes a more immediate solution to the more immediate problem of sexual anomie. According to Durkheim, sexual or "conjugal" anomie causes human misery and death, and "its cause," in turn, "is divorce." Sexual anomie and the attendant suffering it engenders can be minimized by prohibiting divorce.

Of course, because of the sexual difference of interest with respect to marriage and divorce, the practice of divorce has deleterious consequences for only one sex: men. In contrast, the possibility of divorce has beneficial consequences for women and even protects them from suicide. Confronted with this life-and-death conflict of interest between men and women, Durkheim unequivocally aligns himself with the interests of men.

Durkheim supports the abolition of divorce, with the object of eradicating sexual anomie, ameliorating the condition of men, and decreasing male suicide. He acknowledges that the same measure will cause deterioration in the condition of women and increase female suicide.

> The only way to reduce the number of suicides due to conjugal anomy is to make marriage more indissoluble. What makes the problem especially disturbing and lends it an almost dramatic interest is that the suicides of husbands cannot be diminished in this way without increasing those of wives. *Must one of the sexes necessarily be sacrificed and is the solution only to choose the lesser of two evils? Nothing else seems possible* as long as the interests of husband and wife in marriage are so obviously opposed. (1951, 384; emphasis added)

Durkheim's specific theory of men, women, sexuality, marriage, and divorce contradicts his general theory of organicism. It represents an exceptional instance of a systematic, group-level conflict within the social body. This concept is tendentially unthinkable within the organicist framework. Yet the inconsistency, once again, concerns women only. Theoretical consistency is easily reestablished once again, on condition that Durkheim's "individuals" are understood as men.

In this case the precept of organic unity refers to the harmony and commonality of interests uniting genuine elements of the social organism—that is, all individual men. Here Durkheim's theory of sexual anomie, suicide, and the (male) individual serves as an example rather than an exception. Women constitute an exception to the theory of organicism and to the theory of sexual anomie. But as soon as women are excluded from the category "individual," the organic theory of the individual and the anomic theory of the individual are internally logical and perfectly compatible.

In patriarchal reality, women are reduced to physical bodies in the service of men and excluded from "the social body" and "the collective consciousness." Excluding women in theory from Durkheim's construction of "society" and his conception of "the individual" conduces to internal, theoretical consistency and in a sense to external, apodictic consistency, as an accurate "representation" of certain "real" social relations if not an accurate explanation of them.

The sexual contradiction of the social principle of organicism, in the form of the battle of the sexes that emerges in *Suicide,* is ostensibly corrected in "Divorce by Mutual Consent." In this later article Durkheim "resolves" the sexual conflict of interest by positing that *women,* immune to social forces and unaffected by social influences, *have no interests.* Yet in different ways *Suicide* and "Divorce by Mutual Consent" illustrate the problematicity as well as the duplicity of the term "individual." When this generic/genderless term is specified, it refers either exclusively to men (*Suicide*) or alternately to men and women ("Divorce by Mutual Consent") and thus serves to conceal intrasocietal, intersexual conflicts between two distinct groups of "individuals."

In *Suicide,* Durkheim's own discovery of the sexually differentiated effects of marriage and divorce signals the sexual specificity of the abstract "individual." He devotes long, eloquent passages to the positive, beneficial influence of marriage and the negative, detrimental influence of divorce on "individuals" and their suicide rates. Of course these "individuals" are men only. Women actually experience the opposite effects, but they are simultaneously conflated into and excluded from the discussion by a singular, gender-neutral word.

Durkheim unconsciously alternates between a masculine and a generic human subject, effectively confusing the two. A neutral, neutered human individual subject is frequently implied, and a masculine individual subject is occasionally specified. For example, in *Suicide* Durkheim writes two dense pages about the effects of marriage and divorce on "individuals" and then qualifies it with the following declaration: "But this consequence of divorce is peculiar to the man and does not affect the wife" (1951, 272).

In "Divorce by Mutual Consent," Durkheim invokes "individuals" in an even more complex way. Two distinctly different types of "individuals" are delineated. For some "individuals" marriage represents oppression, and divorce represents liberation from marriage. For other "individuals," sexual anomie represents oppression, and marriage represents liberation from sexual anomie.

This contradictory usage suggests that Durkheim has not effectively neutralized the sexual conflict of interest. Men and women have disappeared, and the conflict between them is submerged. But men and women reemerge, and the opposing interests they embody resurface, in the guise of dichotomous, diametric sets of "individuals."

The contradiction between antithetical sets of "individuals," with antithetical relationships to marriage and divorce, is resolved when some "individuals" are read as women. Specifically, the abstract "spouses" and genderless "individuals" whose interests clash with marriage and society and demand divorce can only mean women. It is perhaps overdetermined then that, in this conflict between individuals/women and marriage/society, Durkheim aligns himself with society. "But there is *another point of view* from which the question must be examined: there is *the interest of the institution of matrimony* itself . . . *divorce must not be extended* in such a way that it contradicts and destroys the principle on which the state of marriage reposes; for then, under pretext of remedying individual evils, it would constitute of itself a *grave social malady*" (1978a, 240–41; emphasis added).

Women must be interpolated as the individuals who suffer from marriage and benefit from divorce. On the other hand, it is obvious that those individuals who benefit from marriage and suffer from divorce are men. Durkheim makes frequent, explicit references to the false (sexual) needs and true (social) needs of men and husbands.[8] Thus, when he says that divorce constitutes "a grave social malady whose repercussions *the individual* would bear" (241), it is clear that he means the *male* individual. "It is true," Durkheim says, "that the preceding facts apply solely to men" (245).

In fact, once "women" and "men" are substituted for "individuals" throughout "Divorce by Mutual Consent," many of the passages make more sense. For example, "The rule of matrimony, like any rule, can be harsh in the way in which it is applied to *individuals* [women]; yet this is not a reason to weaken it. The *individuals* themselves [men] would be the first to suffer for it" (252). Or again, "Thus a measure, the goal of which is to lessen the moral miseries of spouses [women], will have the result of demoralizing them [men] and detaching them [men] further from life" (248).

A rereading of "Divorce by Mutual Consent" indicates that in Durkheim's view marriage is a positive phenomenon and divorce is a negative phenomenon. Overtly this is because marriage is good for men and divorce is bad for men, while women are unaffected and disinterested. From another perspective, this is because the allied interests of marriage and society and some individuals (men) take precedence over the interests of other individuals (women). From this perspective, "Divorce by Mutual Consent" reaches precisely the same conclusion as *Suicide.*

In *Suicide,* Durkheim theorizes that men and women are different and opposed with respect to each other and with respect to marriage and divorce. Yet in *Suicide* he uses the term "individual" exclusively to represent men. In "Divorce by Mutual Consent" Durkheim theorizes that men and women are different but united with respect to each other, marriage, and divorce. Women have no interests, so the interests of women and men are no longer opposed. Yet in this work Durkheim uses the term "individual" to represent, alternately, women and men. Once again the confusion can be dispelled if Durkheim's "individual" is universally understood as a masculine individual; if Durkheim's individuals are seen as men. In that case Durkheim's theory of suicide becomes coherent, his theory of sexual anomie becomes coherent, *Suicide* is reconciled with "Divorce by Mutual Consent," and the interests of men ("individuals") are upheld at the expense of the interests of women (nonindividuals).

The Theory of Social Determinism

Durkheim's work is organized by a pervasive and coherent theory of social determinism. The ubiquitous battle between the individual and society is fixed, and society always prevails. The individual is "determined" by society. This relationship of "determinism" between society and the individual has several meanings for Durkheim. In the first instance it is a negative relationship, a relationship of social control. Durkheim conceptualizes social control in three ways: power, force, and socialization. In the second instance social determinism is a positive relationship between society and the individual, a relationship of social constitution. Society is the "nourishing mother" from which individuals derive "the whole of our moral and intellectual substance" (1961, 92).

The striking feature of Durkheim's social determinism, in both its positive and negative, constitutive and controlling manifestations, is that it is absolute. In all its modes and aspects, social determinism is necessary, inevitable, inescapable. The individual "cannot evade" collective ways of thinking and acting.

In the first place, the individual cannot escape social control. The group tends "of necessity" to subordinate its individual parts, which are "unable *not* to fall under its domination" (1957, 60). Social rules are molds in which individual behavior is "inevitably" shaped and "must" run. Social forces determine individual behavior "with the same degree of necessity as physical forces" (1965b,

260). Social laws are "as necessary as physical laws" (1888, 25–27). With respect to "supraorganic life," society "determines, and it rules what is left undetermined" (1958, 202).

The individual cannot escape social control, and without social constitution the individual is "nothing"; the human mind is a "huge void"; consciousness is "empty." Without social construction, the individual is nothing more than an "empty place." Without social determinism, the individual does not exist, or does not exist as a human being. Without society, the individual "could not raise himself beyond his own level . . . the level of animal nature": "Take away from man all that has a social origin and nothing is left but an animal on a par with other animals. It is society that has raised him to this level above physical nature" (1957, 60).

Durkheim's theory of social determinism is one of his most consistent and systematic theories. He occasionally appears to contradict himself and to take individualist and voluntarist positions. Yet these appearances are deceiving. For Durkheim, human freedom is reduced to a conscious and voluntary compliance with imperative social mandates. Human individuality is reduced to an elaborate development of the social dimension of the individual, which Durkheim calls "personality." Individuals can at most attempt to rebel against the social order, but such rebellion is, both immediately and ultimately, "futile and fruitless." Social determinism is completely inescapable for individuals, without exception. Except, of course, women.

Women are not socially determined in any of the ways that individuals are. They are not subject to social power; they are not subjects of imperious social domination; they challenge the absolute sovereignty of society. Women are, equally, unaffected by social forces. In the first place, their instincts are physical rather than social. "Woman" is "a more instinctive creature than man" and is governed "naturally" by the "organism" (1951, 272). In the second place, women exist outside the social environment. Woman lives "outside of community existence" (215–16). She "does little more than look on from a distance" at social life (385).

In the third place, women are immune to social forces conceived of as laws of nature or laws of cause and effect. For example, women are immune to both the positive effects of marriage and the negative effects of divorce (1978a). Similarly, women are immune to the modern social pressure to commit suicide. They "are much less involved than men in collective existence," thus "they feel its influence—good or evil—less strongly" (1951, 299). Again, the low crime rate among women in modern society flouts the modern tendency to deviance. "This is because the causes are social, and women . . . by not participating as directly as men in the collective life, submit less to its influence and experience less of its various consequences" (1980, 409). Women are not impelled by social causes to commit deviant acts. Nor do they refrain from them for social reasons; their low crime rates merely reflect a "lack of opportunity." The existence of women suggests that social laws, unlike natural laws, are not universal.

As an external force, society does not have effectivity for women. It does not compel, control, or constrain them. At the same time, social forces are not internalized by women. Women are "less penetrated" by community existence, "less impregnated with sociability" (1951, 215). They continue to be governed by biological forces and natural instincts because they are not socialized. They are not ruled internally by individualized forms of social forces, the distinctively human manifestation of instincts. The human moment has not occurred for women.

Women are not socially determined in a negative sense; they are not controlled by society. Women are not socially determined in a positive sense either; they are not constituted by society. The social constitution of the individual involves the transformation of a physical creature into a mental and moral being. Mental and moral phenomena are exclusively social in origin. Logically, since women are asocial, they are characterized by a mental and moral deficiency or lack. Women "have no great intellectual needs" (1951, 272). In general, women's "mental life is less developed" (166). They are specialized in the "affective functions" as opposed to the "intellectual functions" of psychic life, which are the province of men (1933, 60). Finally, consistently, "Woman's moral sense is less deeply rooted than man's" (1980, 414).

It is human nature, the nature and fate of the human individual, to be social, socialized, socially determined. Yet women are intransigently asocial, unsocialized, socially undetermined. The difference between women and individuals resolves once again into the difference between women and men. There are "natural differences" in the "nature" or "constitution" of men and women; a "flagrant" "psychological inequality" divides the sexes. Specifically, the two sexes "do not share equally in social life" (1951, 385–86): "Man is much more highly socialized than woman. His tastes, aspirations and humor have in large part a collective origin, while his companion's are more directly influenced by her organism" (385). Conversely, it is a "truth" that "woman's nature is less strongly socialized than man's" (1980, 414): "Woman has had less part than man in the movement of civilization. She participates less and derives less profit" (1933, 247). In fine, men are, essentially, "the product of society," while women are, essentially, "the product of nature" (1951, 386).

In conceptualizing women as asocial organisms, Durkheim not only contra-

83 ■

dicts his theory of social determinism. He also contradicts his related theory, "the dualism of human nature." According to this theory, all individuals have two dimensions, a material, biological dimension and an ideational, social dimension. On the one hand, the individual is equivalent to a body. On the other hand, the individual is equivalent to a soul: a mind and a conscience—an *esprit*. The individual qua individual is purely physical, a natural creature, an animal. The individual qua human being is primarily a psychic being, a mental and moral entity, a social creation. This dualism can be understood as the dualism between the individual as organism and the individual as personality.[9]

Durkheim views the individual as the site of conflict between its own individual, animal nature and its social, human nature, which derives from the collective. To some extent Durkheim identifies the individual self or body as the profane source of individual and social problems (egoism, anomie) and the collective self or soul as the sacred source of solutions to these problems (integration, regulation).[10]

There is a pronounced tension in Durkheim's thought between his theory of the dualism of human nature and his most rigorous formulations of social determinism. The theory of the dualism of human nature associates individuals with bodies and bodies with deviance and social problems. The rigorous version of social determinism views society as responsible for deviance as well as conformity, social problems as well as social solutions.

The theory of sexual anomie is consistent with Durkheim's "hard" theory of social determinism, but not with his theory of the dualism of human nature. According to the theory of sexual anomie, the morbid passion for the infinite stems not from the individual body but from the social mind. That is why sexual anomie is exclusively a male problem—only males are susceptible to mental—that is, social—problems and mental—that is, social—solutions.

Conversely, women's immunity from sexual anomie is consistent neither with the dualism of human nature nor with radical social determinism. Women have neither physically nor socially based problems and neither require nor benefit from social solutions. Women's sexual desires are purely biological, and these natural needs are naturally regulated and satiated. As opposed to men, women, like animals, have both physical—that is, organic—problems and physical—that is, organic—solutions.

Men can be problematic, for themselves and society, through excessive individualism (egoism, anomie) and insufficient socialization (integration, regulation). Alternatively, they can be problematic, for themselves and society, through pathological socialization (social "currents" of egoism and anomie) that is not sufficiently mitigated by normal socialization (social tendencies to integration and regulation). Women, despite the fact that they are unsocialized, do not pose problems either for themselves or for society. They require no socialization, and they are immune to negative social currents.

Durkheim's theory of women contradicts his theory of socialization in both its dualistic and its deterministic variants. There are two possible resolutions. First, Durkheim's individual can be seen as a universal—male or female—individual. Thus both men and women are characterized by a universal human nature; male and female individuals are universally split into a physical body and a social mind; male and female individuals alike can deviate either because their profane bodies are insufficiently socialized or because pathological social forces predominate over normal social forces.

An alternative, implicit image is suggested by Durkheim's theories of women and sexuality. In this image, the *dualism* of human nature becomes the *duality* of human nature. Human nature is not a bifurcated unity. Human nature is simply bifurcated. The physical/mental, natural/social polarity within individuals is transformed into a physical/mental, natural/social polarity between individuals. The dualism unsocialized/socialized within men reemerges as a duality between socialized men and unsocialized women.

Men are completely mental, even in their sexuality, and completely social, even in their antisocial anomie. Women are completely physical, even in their sexuality, and completely natural, even in their pro-social regulation. Women are identified with the physical individual, with the organism: with the body, instinct, and nature. Men, or generic individuals, are identified with the social individual, with the personality: with the triumph of mind over body, morality over instinct, society over nature.

With the appearance of women, human nature disappears into male nature and female nature. Human nature becomes human natures, which is to say that "human" nature does not exist. Or human nature is invested entirely in men, whose nature is quintessentially human: mental and social. Conversely, human nature is divested from women, whose nature is quintessentially nonhuman: physical and natural. Women represent the side of human nature that men and society seek to repress and dominate. Women embody the individual, animal, physical, natural, *profane* aspect of life that collective, human, mental, moral, *sacred* male society transcends. Men are human. Women are Other.[11]

There is a contradiction between Durkheim's theory of women and his theories of socialization. Durkheim's theory of women excludes socialization; his theories of socialization exclude women. But his theories of socialization are not *falsified* by his theory of women, they are merely *specified*. In light of Durkheim's definition of women, the dualism of "the individual" refers exclusively to the dualism of men. In light of Durkheim's definition of socialization, the socialization of "the individual"—whether normal or pathological—refers exclusively to the socialization of men.

Women are thus strictly associated with individuality in its negative, asocial, animal sense. Yet they are denied individuality in its positive, social, human sense. Thus the pair regulation/rebellion, in which Durkheim frames his discussions of the individual/society relation, is meaningless with respect to women. Women are not regulated by society as "individuals" are. Yet they have no freedom, either: they do not enjoy the liberty through social regulation that "individuals" enjoy.[12] They do not attempt to rebel against social regulation as "individuals" do. And they are not privy to the ultimate human liberty: conscious consent, enlightened obedience to social laws. Women are not socially regulated, and they are not socially free. They are naturally determined rather than socially determined. And for Durkheim this means they are not truly human.[13]

Women are individuals as physical bodies. But they are not individuals as social personalities. The only other nominal humans without personalities are primitives and children. The "civilized man" is "a person in greater measure than the primitive; the adult than the child" (1961, 73). Childhood is the period when "the individual, in both the physical and moral sense, does not yet exist." The child is "not . . . a person wholly formed—not a complete work or a finished product—but . . . a becoming, an incipient being, a person in the process of formation" (1979, 150). Likewise, in primitive society "our individuality is nil . . . our personality vanishes . . . the individual does not appear" (1933, 130). In the primitive stage of evolution, the individual personality "does not exist" (1933, 166n).

Predictably, Durkheim compares women to both children and primitives.[14] Women, like children, are asocial. They are not controlled by social forces. "Women . . . are much less involved than men in collective existence; thus they feel its influence—good or evil—less strongly. So it is with old persons and children, though for other reasons" (1951, 299). Women, like primitives, are uncivilized. They are not constituted by social forces. "Woman had less part than man in the movement of civilization. She participates less and derives less profit. She recalls, moreover, certain characteristics of primitive natures" (1933, 247). The "female form" represents "the aboriginal image of what was the one and only type from which the masculine variety slowly detached itself" (1933, 57).

Women are like children and people in lower societies, where "the physical man . . . tends to be the whole of man" (1951, 215). The difference between women and children or primitives is that, unlike the latter, women are not destined to be either socialized or civilized. "The female sex will not again become more similar to the male; on the contrary, we may foresee that it will become more different" (1951, 386). Through maturation and evolution men become, individually and collectively, progressively more socialized and more civilized—more mental and moral, more human. Women remain, both individually and collectively, in a state of nature.

When Durkheim refers to the individual positively, as in the "cult of the individual," he specifies that he is referring to "the individualized forms of collective forces." Thus he is referring to the personality, the social individual, the human individual—to Man.[15] In the quintessential formulations, "man is man only because he lives in society" (1957, 60) and "a man is only a man to the degree that he is civilized" (1953, 56; 1965b, 243). Durkheim is not accidentally or archaically substituting a masculine subject for a generic one. Durkheim says that "the individual is a product of society" (1969, 28). What he means, quite literally, is that "man is . . . a product of society" (1961, 69).

The Theory of Liberalism

The debate over whether Durkheim's social theory is essentially conservative, liberal, or radical has never been conclusively resolved.[16] However, there is at least one subject on which his ideological position is undebatable and undeniable. With respect to economic stratification, Durkheim's formulations are purely, unambiguously, and categorically liberal. They center on the essential liberal construct, the "individual."

Durkheim believes that humans are characterized by inherent differences in ability, both quantitative and qualitative. He further believes that this differentiation occurs at the individual level. Thus he opposes the conservative (feudalist) notion that the differentiation of ability occurs at the group level. He also opposes the more radical (and more Durkheimian) notion that ability is learned rather than innate.[17]

As a consequence of his liberal belief in the inherent and individual nature of ability, Durkheim supports the liberal ideal of individual mobility through equal opportunity. In sociological parlance, Durkheim believes in an achievement, or class, system of stratification as opposed to an ascriptive, or caste, system. Individuals should be free to choose the occupations for which they are best suited according to their inherent abilities. They should not be assigned to occupations on the basis of their group status. The former is a natural allocation mechanism corresponding to natural individual differences. The latter is an artificial mechanism corresponding to nonexistent group differences.

Durkheim's ideal stratification system would represent a perfect correspondence between the hierarchical orders of: individual ability, occupational requirements, and social value. Ideally these parallel structures would be in perfect alignment with one additional structure: the hierarchical order of material remuneration. Each individual's natural talent would be utilized in the appropriate occupation; each occupation would be filled by appropriate individuals according to the rigor of its requirements, valued relative to its contribution to society, and rewarded commensurately on these three bases (ability, difficulty, functionality).[18]

Durkheim fully recognized that this ideal condition did not predominate in his own social milieu. Thus he devotes a chapter to this issue in book 3 of *The Division of Labor.* Book 3 concerns "abnormal forms" of the division of labor, and the abnormal form in question is "the forced division of labor." According to Durkheim, the division of labor is "forced" whenever individuals occupy positions that do not correspond to their native abilities. This occurs primarily through "external inequalities"; in other words, because of unequal opportunity.

External inequalities are inequalities in the conditions of competition. They are "external" because they are unrelated to inherent individual merit, an "internal" condition. These external, artificial inequalities, such as the anachronistic institutions of ascription and inheritance, must be eliminated. It is only when external inequalities are suppressed and the conditions of competition are equal that "internal inequalities"—inborn, natural, individual inequalities of ability—can be expressed in the occupational structure.

When no external inequalities exist to skew the process, individuals can occupy the positions to which they are naturally suited and receive the remuneration to which they are naturally entitled. Under conditions of equal opportunity, individual employees conclude "fair" or "just" exchanges with individual employers, manifest in "fair" or "just" contracts of employment. To the extent that this occurs, a "fair" or "just" division of labor, as opposed to a "forced" division of labor, prevails.

Durkheim's conception of the economic order of individuals is perfectly consistent, and perfectly consistent with liberal principles. Yet this internal, theoretical congruity—as well as this external, ideological congruity—is effectively challenged by the consideration of women. Women do not fit into

Durkheim's coherent, liberal socioeconomic scheme. With respect to women Durkheim maintains a self-contradictory, and essentially conservative, theory. His theory of women is a theory of caste.

In terms of ability, women are not differentiated, as individuals, from each other. Instead they are differentiated, as a group, from men. Men exist as individuals because they are structurally differentiated from each other. This differentiation enables men, as individuals, to assume a wide variety of specialized functions. Men have diverse, individualized "natures" and therefore they are naturally suited to an infinity of diverse occupations. Conversely, women exist only as a group because they are structurally differentiated only from men. The structural isomorphism of women relegates them, as a group, to one singular function. Women have a uniform group "nature" and therefore they are naturally suited to one uniform occupation.

Women are unified, and distinguished from men, by their morphological nature or structure, which is asocial. Because of their asocial "constitution," women are generally amoral and nonintellectual. Women's inherent abilities therefore exist only as residual categories: as presocial or natural abilities. The innate and collective structure of women is biological and emotional. Because of this structure or nature, which is particular to women and universal among them, women are uniquely suited to a unique function: the function of the family.[19]

The significance of these formulations for the present discussion is that women are considered as one homogeneous entity: they constitute a primitive, undifferentiated collectivity. Women are identical in nature or structure and therefore can only be identical in occupation or function. Similarly, the occupation to which women are predisposed by nature is an undifferentiated one. The private, domestic, "interior," "affective" familial function is singular. Women inhabit a mechanical society.

Conversely, men are differentiated both from women, as a group, and from each other, as individuals. As social, intellectual beings, men are disqualified from specializing in domestic life. Beyond that, however, their occupational aspirations are limited only by their innate aptitudes. The public, social, exterior, intellectual functions for which men are qualified exist, like men themselves, in infinite heterogeneity. Man is different from woman. Individual men are different from other individual men.

Women are not individuals for two reasons. In the first place, they exist as an undifferentiated group. Women form a primitive society "where the individual, as such, does not exist." In the second place, women are not part of Durkheim's liberal conception of modern society. Unlike men, women are not characterized by inherent, individualized, intellectual skills that can be exchanged in the marketplace for wages and applied to diverse "functions of utility."

The sexual differentiation of structure (nature, or constitution) causes a sexual specialization of function. This sexual division of labor effectively excludes women from the social division of labor. *The Division of Labor in Society* concerns *organic* solidarity among structurally differentiated and functionally specialized *individuals* in the public sphere. *The Division of Labor in Society,* then, is about the society of men.

This reading of Durkheim generates a theoretical coherence of its own, but one that Durkheim himself did not recognize or elaborate. This reading exposes the theory, merely implicit, of a dual society—of a contradictory social unity. The incorporation of Durkheim's theory of women into his social theory can be achieved not only through the theoretical integration of women into society as "individuals," but also through the theoretical division of society into two separate spheres.

Durkheim's theory would thus contain two internally coherent structures: a theory of men and a theory of women. These two theoretical structures would correspond to two internally consistent structures in society: the male world and the female world. The male world is the world Durkheim refers to as "society." It is the social sphere properly speaking, which is to say it is the arena of the social as opposed to the natural—the arena of the intellectual and the moral, of civilization, of humanity. It is the public, intellectual, productive world, which is generally identified as society in its totality. It is simultaneously the world of liberalism, individualism, egalitarianism, and capitalism. At the same time, it is the modern world of individual heterogeneity, the division of labor, and organic solidarity.

Connected to this prominent, visible, social, male world is a second dimension, an underside of society. The female realm is an asocial area within society. It is the realm of the natural as opposed to the social: the biological, the instinctual, the physical, the animalistic. It is the private, affective, reproductive realm, a localized segment of the total society: the family. Simultaneously, the female world is a feudal, patriarchal world of caste and conservatism. And finally, the female world is a primitive world of individual homogeneity, identity of labor, and mechanical solidarity. In relation to the "society" of men, the world of women is: not a society, since it is not social; part of society, since it is the institution of the family; a feudal society; and a primitive society.

The two separate spheres of men and women are thus diametric, or contrary, and yet they are interconnected and mutually dependent.[20] The world of women does not resemble the world of men, which Durkheim calls society, but it is at the same time a necessary condition of that society. The modern, male capitalist society of individuals contains within itself its own essential and integral antithesis. The public sphere necessarily implies its own inverse, the private sphere. The category "individual" or man automatically engenders its own negative image: woman.

Consequently there are three distinct societies within modern society. There is the society of women, which is a primitive society characterized by relations of resemblance and mechanical solidarity. There is the society of men, which is a modern society of differentiated and specialized individuals. This individual division of labor generates organic, individual solidarity. These two spheres, male and female, public and private, are conjoined by "conjugal society," the intermediate society formed by structurally differentiated and functionally specialized groups: women and men. It is characterized by a sexual division of labor and therefore by organic, sexual solidarity. The second of these societies, the society of men, is what Durkheim refers to when he speaks of "the division of labor in society." He neglects the conjugal society that organically joins men to women and the mechanical society that mechanically joins women to each other. Furthermore, Durkheim neglects to distinguish between "individuals," by which he means men, and women, who are not individuals.

This chapter has explored several sites where the consistency and coherence of Durkheim's social theory breaks down into contradiction. These contradictions, otherwise latent, emerge immediately upon a confrontation between Durkheim's social theory and his theory of women. The sites considered here involve various Durkheimian conceptions of the "individual": the organically unified nature of the cell-like individual; the socially determined nature of the human individual; and the innately differentiated nature of the modern, specialized individual.

In each of these cases Durkheim's theoretical construction of women diverges from his theoretical construction of individuals. There are two possible interpretive responses to this paradoxical situation. The first is to acknowledge theoretical contradiction—error—in the totality of Durkheim's work. The concept of the "individual" is a genderless concept, intended to include all human beings, female as well as male. Durkheim's sexist views of women represent a blind spot—a subconscious, ideological intrusion, an anomalous, disruptive presence in an otherwise unified theoretical structure.[21]

Women should be understood in the Durkheimian framework not as different, but as the same; they should be understood as "individuals." Durkheim can be corrected, properly understood, if he is rewritten, if his theoretical/ ideological women are rewritten. Durkheim's sexist ideologies must merely be erased; the concept of women must merely be assimilated into the abstract concept of the individual. This rewriting of Durkheim will restore his theoretical integrity—will, in effect, save Durkheim from himself, from contradictions that are essentially inadvertent.

There is another possible interpretive response, however, one that would effectively resolve the contradiction and yet leave every dimension of Durkheim's theoretical structure intact. According to this approach, the concept of the individual would be understood as referring exclusively to men, as excluding women. Durkheim's theory of the individual would retain its internal consistency because the incongruous, contradictory element—women—would be external to it. Thus individuals would be men, and women would be something other.[22]

The first interpretation is the standard reading of Durkheimian theory and capitalist society. Durkheim accurately describes the public sphere of men in liberal, individualistic terms. But his theory and that reality are characterized by "survivals" of conservatism, castism, feudalism, and patriarchy—survivals that are limited to the domain of women. According to this interpretation, Durkheim's theory is aberrant and flawed, but understandably so. Durkheim was subject both to the persistence of archaic social ideology and to the persistence of archaic social reality. These persistencies explain his theoretical errors.

Similarly, capitalist society is aberrant and flawed, but temporarily so. Capitalism is subject to the persistence of feudalism. It is this persistence that explains the dual male and female spheres. However, the essence of capitalism is systematic liberal individualism, or equal opportunity. The development of capitalism therefore inevitably involves the progressive extension of individualism to all individuals. The logic of capitalism will eventually eliminate the logic of feudalism, and the two spheres will become one.

The second interpretation is a new reading of Durkheimian theory and of capitalist society. According to this interpretation, Durkheim accurately describes the dual nature of capitalism: the necessary coexistence of a male, public, social sphere of individuals and a female, private, separate sphere of caste. The essence of capitalism is duality. The development of capitalism therefore inevitably involves maintaining this duality. The logic of capitalism is the logic of "man's world" and "woman's world," and never the twain shall meet.

The existence of these alternative interpretations poses a dilemma whose resolution is crucial to a correct and comprehensive understanding of Durkheim's thought. Is Durkheim's sexism an anomaly, an ideologically motivated mistake, a true theoretical contradiction? Does his theory of capitalism differ from Wollstonecraft's, Taylor's, or Mill's, for example, because Durkheim is blinder, more conservative, more of a sexist? Or does the sexual dualism in Durkheim's thought represent an extraordinary insight, a clear and brilliant vision of the true and essential sexual dualism in capitalist society?

The significance of this dilemma extends beyond Durkheimian social theory, however, since it bears on the nature of capitalist society. In many ways Durkheim was a sentient and prescient student of capitalism. He went beyond the inherent limitations of classic liberalism and its description and defense of atomistic, individualistic, laissez-faire capitalism. He foresaw and advocated the social and statist reforms endemic to late capitalism. Durkheim was a quintessential and prototypical neoliberal, a neoliberal ahead of his time.

Durkheim's social theory reflects or captures capitalist society with remarkable breadth and perspicacity. This specific theoretical construction must be interrogated, therefore, about the place of women in this specific social structure. It is ironic, but nonetheless true, that contemporary feminist theory must investigate Durkheim, but not simply as a nemesis, not simply as an object of ideological critique. Feminist theory must investigate Durkheim as part of its ongoing investigation of the relationship between capitalism and patriarchy.

Chapter 5

THEORIES
OF RACE,
CLASS,
AND SEX

▪ The fundamental logic of Durkheim's social theory is the logic of organicism. Durkheim conceives of society as a vast organism, the apotheosis of nature. Like all organisms, the social organism comprises cells and organs: in this case, human individuals and institutions. Like all organisms, the social organism operates as a set of essential structures performing a set of essential functions. The fundamental relationships between and among society, individuals, and institutions are relationships of unity, mutual necessity, and mutual benefit.

The only division within the social organism thus conceived is the division of labor. The only change within this social organism is evolutionary development. Social division and social evolution are in fact one simultaneous and identical process: the process of specialization. The only problem in the specialized social organism is organization: the reunification, through integration and regulation, of increasingly differentiated social cells and organs.

It is not surprising, then, that race, class, and sex are not featured prominently in Durkheim's work. Race, class, and sex are social divisions that are irreducible to structural-functional specialization. Race, class, and sex are sources of social change that is irreducible to evolutionary differentiation. They pose social problems that are irreducible to the problem of specialized parts in an organic whole. They are not elements of an organicist model, and they rarely appear in Durkheimian sociology.

On the other hand, race, class, and sex are not completely invisible in Durkheim's work. They appear, but only momentarily, and only to be resolved into the terms of organicism. The confrontational social groups represented by these categories vanish and reemerge as individuals confronting society. The conflictual relations between races, classes, and sexes vanish and reemerge as functional relations among specialized occupational organs. Groups are recast as individuals; division is recast as specialization; conflictual categories are recast as occupational categories.

Durkheim essentially reformulates race, class, and sex to render them compatible with the organic model. He recuperates them for organicism, for his own social theory. What is more, he presents this theoretical recuperation as a historical transformation. To Durkheim's way of thinking, he is performing an act of scientific description rather than an act of theoretical distortion. According to Durkheim, races and classes (if not sexes) *are* disappearing. They are dissolving into the emergent categories of modernity: the individual cells and occupational organs of the social organism.

Race and Racism

The Disappearance of Race

In *The Division of Labor in Society* and *Suicide,* Durkheim resolves the category of race into the categories "individual" and "society." In the first place, he traces the decline of suprasocietal races, the major prehistoric races, which were limited in number and extensive in size. These "great primitive and fundamental races" ultimately lose "almost all individuality" (1951, 84). The original races eventually disintegrate into distinct groups that are smaller and more numerous. Most important, the new groups are social rather than biological in nature. Human beings are no longer subdivided into races, but into societies.[1] Racial resemblances are replaced by "moral resemblances," which distinguish "civilizations rather than races." Human varieties are increasingly varieties of "human culture" (1933, 309).[2] Racial species become social species.

In the second place, Durkheim traces the decline of intrasocietal races, the races that either parallel or transect societies. These races eventually disintegrate into distinct individuals, destroyed by the individual variation and diversity that accompany the division of labor. "Race and individuality are two contradictory forces which vary inversely with each other" (1933, 304). Individuality, of course, expands with the evolutionary development of society; individual differentiation is a necessary concomitant of functional specialization. Therefore race is destined to be surpassed as a category of human life.

Durkheim sees the category of race progressively superseded by social similarity, on the one hand, and individual difference on the other. Race "no longer represents merely the most general branches of the species, the natural and relatively unchangeable divisions of humanity, but every sort of type" (1951, 84). Race becomes synonymous with nation, and the nation is not actually a race but a society. Resemblances among human beings become cultural and therefore social resemblances. The physical resemblances of race disappear.[3] Furthermore, human resemblance is shattered by individuation, a process essential to the division of labor and fatal to the division of race. In modern society, Durkheim concludes, "the word 'race' no longer corresponds to anything definite" (1951, 85).

The disappearance of race and the emergence of the individual and society are necessary aspects of social evolution. Race is a vital aspect of simple society, where the division of labor is either nonexistent or rudimentary. In contrast, complex or organized society is characterized by a sophisticated division of labor and the nascent dualism of the individual and society.

Simple or "lower" societies are societies of simple, general, and physical functions requiring simple, general, and physical aptitudes. These aptitudes are transmitted genetically, and it is precisely this hereditary transmission that constitutes race. In the most primitive societies, with no division of labor, race is coextensive with the entire society. In societies with a rudimentary division of labor, the hereditary transmission of abilities creates diverse races within a given society, each genetically suited to a particular function.[4]

These occupational races, or "occupational types," form the natural foundation for the social institutions of caste and class.[5] The natural distribution of ability according to race is reflected or expressed in the social distribution of functions according to caste.[6] The caste system is thus "founded in the nature of the society." It "expresses . . . the immutable manner in which occupational aptitudes distribute themselves" (1933, 377).

Simple functions are expressed in simple structures; simple structures are expressed in hereditary "types"—occupational "organs" or races, which are expressed in the caste system. Finally, the caste system is expressed in cultural beliefs of racial/caste/class difference and inequality. These beliefs are problematic if they persist in modern society as anachronistic prejudices. However, in "lower" societies they are perfectly natural and true. "It is impossible . . . that so general an error be a simple illusion and correspond to nothing in reality" (1933, 307).

The declining significance of race is a product of the declining significance of heredity, which in turn is a product of social evolution. Durkheim elaborates this process in book 2, chapter 4, of *The Division of Labor*. In the first place, there is a relative decline in the influence of heredity, owing to the relative increase in "additions" to it, or social acquisitions. The new activities generated by the division of labor are now complex rather than simple, specialized rather than general, and mental rather than physical. Thus they are primarily learned; they require "technique and knowledge," which are socially rather than genetically transmitted.

In the second place, there is an absolute decline in the influence of heredity owing to its increasing "indeterminacy."[7] Heredity becomes increasingly indeterminate for three reasons. First, the role of instinct in determining human behavior is gradually eclipsed by the role of intelligence.[8] Second, there is a progressive "dispersion and effacement" of the "hereditary type" owing to increasing individual variations. Finally, Durkheim maintains that it is "the average type" that is transmitted by heredity, and that the average type becomes increasingly diffuse.[9]

The division of labor both facilitates and necessitates the decline of heredity and race. Complex society entails extensive occupational specialization and incessant functional adaptation. Therefore the homogeneity of race and the inflexibility of heredity, along with their institutional expressions, must be surpassed if modernity is to prevail. Both the natural and the social structures of simple society must be transcended. "For the division of labor to be able to develop, men had to succeed in shaking off the yoke of heredity, progress had to break up castes and classes. The progressive disappearance of these latter tends to prove the reality of this emancipation, for we cannot see how, if heredity had lost none of its claims over the individual, it could have been weakened as an institution" (1933, 308).

Higher society, like lower society, is an interrelated set of expressive levels. But the natural foundation, the underlying substructure or "conditions of existence" in modern society is the division of labor. Complex, organized society by definition comprises multiple occupational functions. It is therefore characterized by individual variation, by structurally differentiated individual cells. Social functions are complex, specialized, and mental. Individual functionaries are indeterminate and variable. Therefore modern structures or organs are fitted to modern functions through social transmission, which acts at the level of the individual.

This distribution of indeterminate individuals to infinitely diverse occupations is reflected in the modern social system of individual mobility or equal opportunity. This institutional order is in turn reflected in the modern belief system—individualistic meritocracy. This entire multilevel, expressive totality is well adapted to the environment because of its internal variation—functional differentiation and structural specialization—and continuously adaptive to its environment because of its internal variability. Social evolution inexorably creates modern society, as inevitable as it is superior. And modern society inexorably destroys hereditary determination and racial similarity.

The social change described by Durkheim, in which race and heredity are vanquished, is a part of a general process of evolution in which society progressively transcends nature.[10] This movement of transcendence has several aspects. First, society surpasses nature (social nature surpasses physical nature) in the mode of *dissimilarity* and *displacement*. This trajectory, from the natural/physical to the social/mental, is marked by the evolution of instinct into intelligence, heredity into culture, race into individuality.[11] Society replaces nature as the basis for the divisions among human groups and as the medium for the transmission of human characteristics. Most crucially, society replaces nature as the primary determinant of human beings. Society supplants the organism and the external environment, instinct and heredity, as the decisive causal "milieu" that produces human behavior. Social causes supersede biological, organic, physical causes in constituting human nature. "Man . . . is dependent upon social causes. . . . In man . . . and particularly in higher societies, social causes substitute themselves for organic causes" (1933, 345–46). Modern society, then, is characterized by the emergence of social determinism through the displacement of nature and natural determinism.

Modern society is simultaneously characterized by the emergence of individuality through the displacement of race and racial determinism. The ascendancy of society as a causal force is paralleled by the ascent of individuals as autonomous entities. Modernity therefore presents an apparent contradiction. However, this is a contradiction that Durkheim easily, if not always explicitly, resolves. The natural is ultimately eclipsed by the social, and the racial is ultimately eclipsed by the individual, because the physical is ultimately eclipsed by the mental.[12] Psychic forces are social forces, external and coercive in relation to individuals. Human individuals are liberated from physical causality as they become increasingly mental beings. But Durkheim equates the mental with the social, and therefore the human, mental individual is a socially determined individual. Modernity involves the emergence of society, the individual, and the psychic life that links them in a relation of determination.

Durkheim theorizes the displacement of the natural by the social, as part of human evolution, in *The Division of Labor*. He substantiates this argument in *Suicide*. In the latter work he establishes that human groups are causal with respect to human behavior and that they are social rather than natural phenomena. Human resemblances are social rather than racial; human types are historical rather than natural; human groups are peoples or societies of peoples rather than races. Civilization rather than blood links people, and "race" either "no longer corresponds to anything definite" or becomes "identical with nationality" (1951, 85). In particular, Durkheim observes that suicide rates are linked to social and not racial categories.[13] Suicide is essentially a mental rather than a physical phenomenon; therefore it is social rather than natural, socioindividual rather than racial.

99 ▪

Social evolution corresponds to the social transcendence of nature in another way. Society (psychic life) progressively surpasses nature (physical life) in the mode of *domination*. "Man . . . can escape nature only by creating another world where he dominates nature. That world is society" (1933, 387). One of the natural conditions that society increasingly vanquishes is inequality. Natural inequalities "are the very negation of liberty." Therefore liberty "results from social action"; it consists in "a conquest of society over nature": "Naturally, men are unequal in physical force; naturally, they are placed under external conditions unequally advantageous. . . . In short, liberty is the subordination of external forces to social forces. . . . But this subordination is rather the reverse of the natural order" (1933, 386–87). Modern society, through the division of labor, creates structurally differentiated individuals and functionally specialized occupational groups. To do so, it must destroy the natural groups that impede individualization, individual mobility, occupational specialization, and equal opportunity. These natural and unequal groups, characteristic of segmental society, include regional groups, families, and races and the social castes and classes that reflect them.

In addition to his abstract treatment of race in *The Division of Labor* and *Suicide*, Durkheim addresses the issue in two important topical articles. Both articles concern the Dreyfus Affair, infamous for its anti-Semitic implications. Durkheim was actively involved in the Dreyfusard cause. In addition, he was Jewish himself and experienced anti-Semitism personally at various periods in his life.[14] It is thus striking that the first of these articles, "Individualism and the Intellectuals" (1969), makes no reference to racism.

"Individualism and the Intellectuals" is an important work. In it Durkheim elaborates a recurrent and difficult theme: the relationship between individualism and collectivism. Durkheim reconciles these two contrary ideals by redefining individualism and equating it with collectivism. What is of even greater interest here, however, is another theoretical maneuver within the same article. The Dreyfus Affair is commonly thought of not only as a conflict over individual rights, but also as a racial conflict, as an instance of French anti-Semitism. Yet Durkheim does not mention race or anti-Semitism in the entire article. In fact, he transforms a concrete political controversy that involves racial issues into an abstract theoretical controversy focused exclusively on the synthesis of individualism and collectivism. He prefaces his article with the following suggestion: "Let us forget the Affair itself. . . . The problem confronting us goes infinitely beyond the current events, and must be disengaged from them" (1969, 20).

Racism as False Consciousness

In "Individualism and the Intellectuals" Durkheim mediates the conflict between individualism and collectivism by resolving individualism into collectivism. In addition, he mediates the conflict between French anti-Semites and French Jews by resolving anti-Semitism into individualism/collectivism. Durkheim denies the intrasocietal problem of group/group conflict, replacing the terms French and Jewish with the terms individual and society. This latter pair is not really a dichotomy and is therefore not really problematic. Thus "Individualism and the Intellectuals" repeats the process of *The Division of Labor* and *Suicide:* it dissolves races of individuals into individuals in society. But it does so in an overdetermined way as well as in a different way.

In fairness to Durkheim, part of the Dreyfus debate did center on the issue of individual rights versus reasons of state. In addition, Durkheim wrote a second article that specifically addresses the issue of anti-Semitism. However, even here he fails to acknowledge intrasocietal, group/group conflict, preferring to understand anti-Semitism as an error or illusion. In fact it is an error or illusion precisely because it posits the existence of races and of intrasocietal group distinctions and conflicts.

This article is a four-page solicited contribution to a collection of reflections on anti-Semitism.[15] In his response, Durkheim calls anti-Semitism in France a "consequence" and "superficial symptom" of "social malaise," a "sign" of "moral disturbance." Anti-Semitism is not a racial problem but is rather a displaced reaction to the "crisis of transition." The crisis of transition is the disruption of social solidarity, the moral and institutional asynchronies and absences occasioned by the dissolution of traditional society. This transformation, in which mechanical solidarity is destroyed before organic solidarity develops, is necessary but painful.

Anti-Semitism is a misplaced symptom of social suffering, a misguided attribution of blame for social problems, a misdirected attempt to cure social ills. It is an exacerbation of the very social disintegration that causes it to appear in the first place. Anti-Semitism responds to social division by further dividing society against itself, into antagonistic social groups, rather than by unifying individuals into one harmonious and comprehensive social collective. In 1899 Durkheim presciently describes anti-Semitism as a form of scapegoating. "When society undergoes suffering, it feels the need to find someone whom it can hold responsible for its sickness, on whom it can avenge its misfortunes" (1899, 345).[16]

Anti-Semitism, as dramatized in the Dreyfus Affair, provides both an illusory cause and an illusory solution to social problems. The public response to the Dreyfus conviction was relief and joyous celebration. "At last they knew whom to blame for the economic troubles and moral distress in which they lived. The trouble came from the Jews. The charge had been officially proved. By this very fact alone, things already seemed to be getting better and people felt consoled" (1899, 345).[17] Anti-Semitism, in effect, represents a false diagnosis, a false prescription, and a false cure for the illness of the social organism. In fact anti-Semitism, "the hatred by some citizens against others," represents the delirious efforts of the stricken social organism to destroy itself precisely by dividing itself into pieces. "One does not let a sick man avenge his suffering on himself by tearing himself apart with his own hands" (1899, 346).[18]

Anti-Semitism is thus an "error," an instance of "public madness." It is a misapprehension of the crisis of transition: it misrecognizes social/individual schisms as racial schisms. It is a misapprehension of the solution to the crisis: it substitutes racial solidarity for social solidarity. It is a misapprehension of Jews in particular, and of the significance of race in general: it projects racial essentialism onto social assimilation and social determinism. "The Jews are losing their ethnic character with an extreme rapidity. In two generations the process will be complete" (1899, 346).[19]

Anti-Semitism is a symptom of social illness, the self-perception and self-mutilation of a sick organism; it is a divisive, antisocial ideology and intervention positing internal and antagonistic racial groups. Anti-Semitism thus precludes true social understanding and true social healing. It is to the science of society as false consciousness is to social consciousness. It is to social solidarity as the symptom of an illness is to the health of an organism.

Recuperation: Durkheim's Antiracism

Durkheim suggests, in effect, three remedies for racism. In the first place, he advocates curing the social malady of which racism is merely a symptom. Racism, like suicide, is a symptom of the moral crisis attendant on the transition to modernity. Thus the cure for racism, like the cure for all social problems, is organic solidarity: effective modern forms of social regulation and integration. The genuine solution for the problem of anti-Semitism, then, consists in treating the moral distress and social malaise that cause it. To destroy anti-Semitism at its source would be "to put an end to this state of disturbance." However, "this is not the work of one day" (1899, 62).

Durkheim thus proposes a second, interim solution, "something immediately possible and urgent that could be done." An immediate and direct attack on anti-Semitism would have three components. The first would be to "repress severely every incitement to hatred by some citizens against others." These "repressive measures" would have the effect of impressing on "public opinion" the odiousness of such a crime. The second component would be the example set by government, which should make its practice conform to its theory (a reference to the Dreyfus Affair) and "take it upon itself to show the masses how they are being misled" (1899, 346).[20] Finally, "men of good sense" should show the courage of their convictions by speaking out and uniting against the "public madness" of anti-Semitism (1899, 62–63).

Finally, Durkheim provides a third, implicit solution. Science must assume its role of demonstrating the true nature and underlying structure of modern society. On the basis of this morphological analysis, science can formulate and prescribe the appropriate superstructural institutions and beliefs. Racism is in one sense merely an anachronistic survival of institutions and beliefs appropriate to caste society. "When the regime of castes has lost juridical force, it survives by itself in customs, and thanks to the persistence of certain prejudices, a certain distinction is attached to some individuals, a certain lack of distinction attached to others, independent of their merits" (1933, 378).

Traditional society is founded on a simple division of labor and the natural determination of group identities through heredity. Therefore it requires institutions of caste and class as well as beliefs and customs reflecting group differences and inequalities. Modern society is founded on a complex division of labor and the social determination of individual diversities through socialization. Therefore it requires institutions of equal opportunity and individual mobility as well as beliefs and customs reflecting individual differences and inequalities. These scientific truths must be invoked to eliminate racism as a "survival"—a superstructure rendered obsolete, incompatible, and dysfunctional by the substructure of modernity. Science must demonstrate that heredity and race have been replaced by society and individuals.

Racism is in another sense the misapprehension of the crisis of transition. It is, as the example of anti-Semitism illustrates, a misdiagnosis of social ills—a self-diagnosis by the debilitated social body, a symptom of moral malaise. The scientific truths of the crisis of transition must be invoked to counter ideological and divisive interpretations such as racism. Science must demonstrate that the real problem is social breakdown rather than race and that individuals must be unified on a social basis rather than divided on a racial basis. Thus on the one hand it is the task of science to prove that the existence of individuals has superseded the existence of race. On the other hand, it is the task of science to prove that the existence of society, the organic solidarity and collective consciousness of those same individuals, should and will supersede the existence of sociomoral crisis.

Durkheim thus opposes racism by denying that race exists. He resolves race into discrete individuals and reduces racism to false ideas. He thus maintains an antiracist position while eliminating the category of race from his social ontology.[21] For Durkheim, racial egalitarianism takes the form of equal opportunity and individual mobility: a recognition in public opinion and social practice of the obsolescence of racial aggregates, castes, and classes. Social reform appears as a dual project: the creation of individual mobility through the destruction of archaic group identities and the destruction of social disintegration through the creation of modern social solidarity. Modern individuals must be different, free, and formally equal. But these different, free, and formally equal individuals must be thoroughly integrated and regulated. Modern society must develop both individual mobility and moral unity.

Class and Socialism

The Disappearance of Class

Durkheim's treatment of class is very similar to his treatment of race. His tendency is to dissolve the conflictual categories of class struggle into the functional categories of organicism: organisms (societies) and their constituent parts, cells (individuals), and organs (occupations). He accomplishes this resolution in three ways.

First, Durkheim conceives of "the" social crisis—the acute and widespread social breakdown that provokes his work—as a *transitional* and *moral* crisis. The social crisis is a "crisis of transition." Therefore it is temporary and abnormal

103 ▪

rather than structural in nature. The social crisis is a crisis of morality. Therefore it concerns the relationship between individuals and society rather than the
relationship between the working class and the capitalist class. Durkheim's
social crisis is significant for what it *is,* a transitional crisis of morality, but also
for what it *is not,* a crisis of capitalism or class society.[22] The solution for
Durkheim's social crisis is thus found in evolutionary development and consol-
idation, rather than in revolutionary division and destruction, of the social
structure of capitalism.

The second way Durkheim eliminates the category of class from his social
ontology is through a focus on "the division of labor in society." Durkheim
concentrates on the differentiation and specialization of the functions of economic production rather than on the differential relations of ownership of the
means of economic production. Therefore he concentrates on complementary
relations among specialized individuals (social cells) and among specialized
occupations (social organs), to the exclusion of conflictual relations between
stratified (owning and nonowning) classes. "Social life can be divided, while
retaining its unity, only if each of these divisions represents a function" (1951,
390).

At the same time that he excludes class relations from consideration, Durkheim subsumes them under relations of specialization. The contrast between
owners and workers is treated as an instance of structural-functional differentiation. Employers and employees are different in that they have different
occupations. They are similar in that both employers and employees are simply
performing particular specialized functions. Durkheim recognizes only one
socioeconomic group intermediate between individuals and society: occupational groups. Economic classes are either excluded by or included in this
structural-functional analysis. In either case, their specific existence is denied.

Because of his understanding of social relations as relations of specialization,
Durkheim believes the problem of social relations can be solved through *organization.* By organization, Durkheim means the coordination, integration,
and regulation of functionally specialized individuals and industries. In other
words, the specialized individual cells need to be organized—integrated and
regulated—within their respective occupational organs. Furthermore, the specialized occupational organs need to be organized—integrated and regulated—
within the larger organism.

The "moral agents" of this socioeconomic organization are "occupational
groups" or "corporations."[23] Internally, each corporation, or occupational organ, would integrate and regulate its constituent individual cells. Externally, all
the various corporations would be related to each other and integrated and

regulated by the state. Local corporations should form "national corporate bodies," and "this whole framework should be attached to the central organ . . . the State" (1957, 38–39). Thus economic life, the "visceral functions" or "vegetative life" of society, would be organized directly by occupational corporations or "nerves"; the corporations in turn would be organized by the state, the "central organ" or brain of the social organism (1957, 30).

Durkheim describes *the* social problem as an absence: an absence of socialization, an absence of integration and regulation, the insufficient presence of society in relation to individuals. The solution to the social problem is therefore a presence: the presence of society in the form of occupational corporations and a national state. These function to organize individuals on the basis of their new occupational similarities and to connect and subordinate individuals/cells, occupations/organs, and economic/visceral functions to the collective society through the state, the central organ or brain of the social organism. "If the problem of the corporation is not the only one demanding public attention, there is certainly none more urgent, for the others can be considered only when this has been solved" (1933, 31).

For Durkheim, the essential social categories of modernity are specialized individuals and occupations. The essential social problem of modernity, therefore, is organic solidarity: the organization, integration, and regulation of differentiated economic structures and functions. The essential social relationships of modernity are contractual relations: the exchange between specialized individuals of their specialized products and services. Thus the third way Durkheim eliminates class struggle from his model of society is through a focus on just contracts and fair exchanges.

Just contracts and fair exchanges characterize a "natural" or "spontaneous" division of labor. There are two dimensions of a spontaneous division of labor. The first concerns the stratified distribution of occupations. In modern society the spontaneous division of labor is the system of individual mobility; natural abilities as well as social functions are distributed at the individual level.[24] The second dimension concerns the stratified remuneration of occupations. In modern society a spontaneous division of labor exists when contracts of exchange reflect the "true" or social value of each social function.[25] Social functions are "of unequal importance" to society and must be unequally rewarded, according to the relative degree of their socially "useful results."[26]

Both dimensions of the spontaneous division of labor are predicated on conditions of "external equality." The fair and just distribution of occupations requires equal opportunity for all individuals. Occupations should be allocated on an individual basis rather than on a group basis. The fair and just remuneration of occupations requires equal bargaining power between employers and employees. Occupations should be remunerated according to the inequality of their social value rather than according to the inequality of the parties to the contract.

Class war, in Durkheim's view, is the result not of private property and structural exploitation, but of unjust contracts and unfair exchanges, or excessive economic demands. Specifically, "class wars" result from two abnormal, pathological, and transient conditions: the "forced division of labor" and "economic anomie": "The lower classes . . . aspire to functions which are closed to them and seek to dispossess those who are exercising these functions. Thus civil wars arise which are due to the manner in which labor is distributed" (1933, 374). The aspirations of the lower classes to higher occupations and higher wages are sometimes legitimate, in instances of a forced division of labor. These same aspirations are sometimes illegitimate, in instances of economic anomie.

An unnatural or "forced" division of labor results from conditions of "external inequality." The distribution of occupations is subject to external inequality when considerations other than the inherent natural abilities of individuals are used to allocate social functions. Specifically, a forced division of labor results when a system of ascriptive distribution survives after differences in occupational ability have shifted from the group level to the individual level. In this instance class wars, as well as class-based "anxiety and pain," reflect the fact that "the distribution of social functions . . . does not respond, or rather no longer responds, to the distribution of natural talents" (1933, 375).

The remuneration of occupations is subject to external inequality when considerations other than the inherent social value of occupations are used to reward social functions. Specifically, a forced division of labor results when a system of inherited wealth creates unequal bargaining power between contracting parties—employers and employees—and therefore promotes unfair exchanges of labor for wages. "In other words, there cannot be rich and poor at birth without there being unjust contracts" (1933, 384). Durkheim argues for the abolition of inheritance, as a survival of primitive communalism and of familial and natural systems of heredity: of caste, class, and race.

A third source of "external inequality" is economic anomie, which affects both the distribution and the remuneration of occupations. In the transitional crisis of morality, individual economic aspirations become limitless. Individuals develop a morbid or pathological "passion for the infinite" with respect to both occupation and income. They strive to occupy functions incommensurate with the natural abilities they possess and to receive rewards incommensurate with the social value of their functions. "The problem must be put this way: to discover through science the moral restraint which can regulate economic life, and by this regulation control selfishness and thus gratify needs" (1958, 240). This moral restraint or "discipline" is required "to make those less favored by nature accept the lesser advantages which they owe to the chance of birth" (1951, 251).

Durkheim advocates "external" equality and accepts inequality of natural ability and inequality of social value as complementary givens. In fact "the progress of the division of labor implies . . . an ever growing inequality." The only viable form of equality is equal opportunity, "equality in the external conditions of conflict" (1933, 379). "To be sure, the unequal merit of men will always bring them into unequal situations in society, but these inequalities are external only in appearance, for they are only the external manifestations of internal inequalities" (1933, 384).

Durkheim acknowledges economic discontent in modern society but views it as a temporary symptom of temporary maladjustments. He attributes the discontent as well as the maladjustments to anachronistic survivals—external inequalities—and transitional phenomena—economic anomie. Furthermore, in focusing on equal opportunity, fair and unfair occupational distributions, just and unjust contracts, Durkheim justifies structural income inequality and ignores systematic exploitation. In focusing on inheritance, he attacks inherited wealth and poverty, alternately ignoring and justifying private ownership of the means of production. Finally, in focusing on economic anomie, Durkheim attacks occupational and material aspirations rather than their lack of fulfillment and targets lower classes rather than upper classes as the source of economic problems.

Socialism as False Consciousness

Ironically, Durkheim rejects socialism for many of the same reasons he rejects racism. Socialism represents a fundamental misinterpretation of society in general and social problems in particular. Because it is based on a false conception of social morphology, it generates false diagnoses of social ills and false prescriptions to remedy them. Like racism, socialism focuses on nonexistent or irrelevant social categories: class analysis is equivalent to racial analysis. Like racism, socialism is divisive: class struggle is equivalent to racial strife. Both ideologies create a scapegoat for social problems: capitalism and capitalists are equivalent to racial inferiority and Jews. Both represent the antithesis of good medicine for the social body.

As noted above, socialism is logically incompatible with Durkheim's organicism. The specificity of Durkheim's "social organism" is complexity (in relation to individual human organisms), not class struggle. The specificity of his "modern social organism" is complexity (in relation to primitive societies), not capitalism. Durkheim's social problem is a moral crisis of transition, not an economic crisis of capitalism. His social solution is organic solidarity, not collective ownership—socialization, not socialism.[27] The social organism requires evolution, not revolution.

- 108

Socialism is equally incompatible with Durkheim's liberalism. For Durkheim, socioeconomic problems revolve around "the forced division of labor" and "external inequalities." They are essentially anachronistic or temporary deviations from liberal capitalism. The solution to these problems consists of "the spontaneous division of labor" and "equality in the external conditions of conflict." This is essentially the perfection, or liberalization, of the capitalist system. Capitalism itself is not a problem, and therefore socialism is not a solution.

An opposition to socialism based on organicism and liberalism is latent and implicit in Durkheimian social theory. However, Durkheim is also explicitly opposed to socialism. His stated rationale for rejecting socialism is that it is not scientific. According to Durkheim, science is essentially and inherently conservative. The scientific method includes the mandate to "treat reality with extreme prudence" and therefore imparts to its practitioners "a conservative attitude" (1933, 35).

Science is conservative because its proper object is existing reality. Its mission is the objective observation of the status quo. The "only job" of science is to "describe and explain what is and what has been." Social science is the study of "what is" in the social realm: the study of "social facts." A scientific social theory "seeks only to express what is or what has been" (1958, 17). In contrast, socialism concerns the "ideal" and the "practical." Because of its focus on "what ought to be," socialism is philosophical rather than scientific (1958, 17, 5). Because of its focus on social change, socialism is "destructive," and "dangerous."

The central difference between social science and socialism is the difference between determinism and voluntarism. Social science is based on the assumption that social facts and physical facts are equally natural facts. Social facts, like physical facts, are essentially "deterministic": preexisting and immutable with respect to human beings. Social science is conservative because it accepts existing social facts as given. "Our reasoning is not at all revolutionary. We are even, in a sense, essentially conservative, since we deal with social facts as such . . . conceive them as deterministic rather than arbitrary" (1938, xxxviii–xxxix). Socialism, on the other hand, is a "destructive" theory, which views social facts as "revocable": "There has been good reason to upbraid certain theories which are thought to be scientific for being destructive and revolutionary: but they are scientific in name only. They construct but they do not observe. They see in ethics, not a collection of facts to study, but a sort of revocable law-making which each thinker establishes for himself" (1933, 35). Socialism is a "dangerous" doctrine, which "sees in social phenomena only the results of unrestrained manipulation, which can in an instant, by a simple dialectical artifice, be completely upset" (1938, xxxix). Socialism aims "to modify what exists." It proposes "not laws, but reforms" (1958, 17).

Socialism is unscientific because it evaluates existing reality—capitalism—negatively. The only scientifically legitimate distinction is between "healthy" or "normal" phenomena and "pathological" or "abnormal" phenomena. The scientific criterion of health or normality is simply widespread existence, or "generality." What is healthy and normal is positive, and what exists is healthy and normal. Conversely, there is only "one intelligible reason for finding certain elements faulty": that is, when they "differ from the average of the others and constitute anomalies in the average type" (1933, 434).[28]

The existence of a phenomenon is an indication of its health and normality. The generality of a phenomenon is proof. This is because in the living, natural world, which includes the social organism, extant and general phenomena are functional. They are necessary and beneficial, adaptive and expressive.[29] At the very least they are neutral. A destructive or negative element is unlikely to appear, and unable to survive, in a living organism or species. Within the framework of organicism, this includes the social organism and social species. Thus socialism ignores the laws of nature when it condemns capitalism, a pervasive social structure. "For socialists it is the capitalist system, in spite of its wide diffusion, which constitutes a deviation from the normal state" (1938, 73–74). On the contrary, the existence, persistence, and prevalence of capitalism demonstrate that it is normal and healthy, positive and functional.

Science is not purely conservative, nor purely *dégagé*, however. It is irreconcilable with revolution, but it is not incompatible with "intervention." Durkheim envisions and supports social intervention, defined strictly as social reform. "When everything is not all it ought to be . . . that . . . will be the time to intervene. But the intervention then is limited; it has for its object, not to make an ethic completely different from the prevailing one, but to correct the latter, or partially to improve it" (1933, 35–36). For Durkheim, social reality is like physical reality; it cannot be radically altered. Social ideals must be very closely related to social reality: "The ideal rests on nothing if it does not keep its roots in reality" (1933, 34). To perfect something in nature is "to make it more like itself": "The only ideal that the human mind can propose is to improve what is. It is in reality alone that one can learn the improvements it demands" (1933, 435).

The social organism is like a physical organism: structural change is undesirable as well as inconceivable. Social structure, like biological structure, is essentially unproblematic. In fact like biological structure it is inherently functional and adaptive. Social problems, like biological problems, result not from structures, but from structural metamorphoses or anomalies. Social problems, like biological problems, are not morphological but transitional or pathological in nature. Therefore social intervention must aim not at structural transformation but at structural realization or restoration. Social problems are growing pains or illnesses; social solutions are spontaneous developments or cures. The intrinsic, natural nature of the social organism cannot and should not be altered. To modify social structure artificially, to change the nature of the social body, would be to destroy society, to kill the collective being.

The ideal is determined by the real. Therefore the ideal must be ascertained by science. Science is knowledge of reality, of "what is." This knowledge is necessary in order to "improve what is." Social science is knowledge of the true nature of society. It is necessary in order to make society "more like itself." The ideal society is actually the normal or healthy state of the extant social organism. The "desirable" is defined by Durkheim as "health and normality" (1938, 75). It is "science alone" that can discern this "state of moral health," which is real and at the same time "ideal" (1933, 34).

With respect to social reform, social science is like biology. It distinguishes the normal and the healthy from the abnormal and pathological in the social organism. "The question does not differ essentially from the one the biologist asks when he seeks to separate the sphere of normal physiology from that of pathological physiology" (1933, 432). Social science, as a practice of social biology, identifies social health and social illness. The state, as a practice of social medicine, realizes social ideals by restoring social health and curing social illness. "The duty of the statesman is no longer to push society toward an ideal that seems attractive to him, but his role is that of the physician: he prevents the outbreak of illnesses by good hygiene, and he seeks to cure them when they have appeared" (1938, 75).

In contrast, socialism is like a symptom of social illness. It is like the "remedies" recommended by a "feverish patient." Socialism is "unscientific." Unlike the realistic social biology of sociologists and the reformist social medicine of statesmen, socialism consists of measures that "the suffering masses of society have spontaneously and instinctively conceived of" (1958, 9). "Socialism is not a science . . . it is a cry of grief, sometimes of anger, uttered by men who feel most keenly our collective malaise. Socialism is to the facts which produce it what the groans of a sick man are to the illness with which he is afflicted, to the needs that torment him" (1958, 7).

Recuperation: Durkheim's "Socialism"

Durkheim renounces socialism as a social theory and as a social system. He rejects it as "false" relative to the "truth" of social science; as false consciousness relative to the true consciousness of Durkheimian structural-functional organicism. At the same time he recuperates socialism and claims it as his own. He does this by redefining socialism until it is compatible with his own views of social theory and social reform. He distinguishes "false" forms of socialism from the essence of socialism—from "true," or Durkheimian, organicist "socialism."[30]

Durkheim identifies several versions or aspects of false socialism. First Durkheim's genuine "socialism" is distinguished from "anarchism." Anarchism is a theory common to laissez-faire liberals and Marxist socialists. The mistake of anarchism is the dual error: "economism" and "individualism." Anarchism attributes central significance to the economic order, to the individual and material realm of human life, to "secular" existence. The correct, Durkheimian view is "social-ism"—that is, that the center and essence of human life is the social order: the collective, moral realm or "sacred" existence, as represented by the central organ of society, the brain—the state—and its central nervous system—occupational corporations.

Second, Durkheim's genuine "socialism" is distinguished from "communism." Communism is a "radical" or "extreme" form of socialism because it demands the abolition of private property. "True" socialism opposes collective or state ownership of property, including the means of production, as "primitive." Communism corresponds to the principles of simple society: collectivism and mechanical solidarity. It contradicts the principles of complex society and the division of labor: individualism, differentiation, specialization, and organic solidarity. Conversely, private property is allegedly a facet of modernity—an instance of individualization and specialization, and therefore a source of mutual dependence and organic solidarity.

Similarly, Durkheim's genuine "socialism" is distinguished from "egalitarianism." Like communism, egalitarianism is a primitive social structure. Social equality corresponds to simple, undifferentiated collective society. In contrast, the division of labor in modern society requires and produces social stratification. The "external" equality that accompanies the division of labor allows for the expression of both natural and social inequality. Modern society, including "socialist" society, is necessarily hierarchical, due to the increasingly unequal abilities of various individuals and the increasingly unequal utility of various functions. The progress of the division of labor thus "implies . . . an ever growing inequality" (1933, 379).

Finally, genuine socialism is distinguished from class struggle. Socialism opposes "class war" as divisive and as antithetical to organic solidarity. True socialism seeks to integrate the various economic organs, including owners and workers—to eliminate economic egocentrism. Economically differentiated groups, as well as economically specialized individuals, must be unified in a common social interest and identity. Furthermore, socialism opposes the promotion of working-class interests as both divisive and futile. True socialism seeks to regulate individuals and groups, including owners and workers—to eliminate economic anomie. Its objective is not to satisfy but to limit the infinite and unrealistic aspirations of the working class in particular. For Durkheim, "socialism" signifies the social-ization of the working class.

Durkheim describes true socialism negatively, by delineating false forms of socialism. He also describes true socialism positively and directly. Socialism is scientific, and Durkheim is a "socialist," if "socialism" is defined in the following way: "Socialism" refers to the "social-ization" of individuals and the economy (1958, 40).[31] It is equivalent to the regulation and integration of specialized individuals and occupations.[32] "Socialism is essentially a movement to organize" (1958, 23). Socialism advocates the connection and subordination of the individual cells and occupational organs of the economy or viscera to the state or brain of the social organism.[33] Individuals are to be organized into occupations, and occupations are to be organized into a social system, through the medium of occupational groups or corporations. Corporations represent the internal and external organization of occupational organs, which are composed of individuals and which in turn compose the social organism.

Socialism is in essence the "reform of the existing order." "All else is communist principle" (1958, 37). Durkheim can define himself as a socialist because he defines "socialist" "science" (or "scientific socialism") as Durkheimian sociology—that is, structural-functional organicism. At the same time, on a political and ontological level Durkheim's true or scientific "socialism" is nothing more or less than his reformist organic solidarity: statist, corporatist capitalism. False socialism is identical with Marxist theory and practice. True socialism is identical with Durkheimian theory and practice.[34]

Sex and Feminism

Feminism as False Consciousness

Durkheim's treatment of sex differs from his treatment of race and class in the sense that he does *not* reduce sexual difference into individual difference; sexually differentiated "men" and "women" are not transformed into discrete and unsexed "individuals." Dichotomous, sexual heterogeneity does not disappear to reemerge as infinite, individual heterogeneity. Durkheim does not dissolve the sexual categories, men and women, in order to absorb them into the organic nexus of individual/occupation/society (cell/organ/organism). Despite this difference, which will be discussed below, there are striking parallels that connect Durkheim's treatment of sex to his treatment of race and class.

In the first place, Durkheim considers feminism, like racism and socialism, a form of false consciousness. Feminism, like racism and socialism, is false. Like them, it is deluded, divisive, and destructive. Like them, it promulgates false solutions, or bad prescriptions, for social ills on the basis of false problematics, or bad descriptions of the social body, and bad diagnoses of its ills. Feminism, racism, and socialism represent bad social practices based on bad social theories. Feminists, like racists and socialists, must be denied any role as social physicians—they must be barred from practicing social medicine—because they are not social biologists: they do not have correct, scientific, Durkheimian knowledge of the morphology and the physiology of the social organism. Durkheim rejects feminism because, like racism and socialism, it is unscientific.

Feminism politically advocates the practice of social similarity and equality between the sexes, based on an ontological theory of natural similarity and equality between them. Similarly, racism and socialism politically advocate the practice of social similarity and equality among individuals, based on an ontological theory of natural similarity and equality among them—within races or between classes. Conversely, Durkheim politically opposes the social practice of sexual similarity and equality, based on his ontological theory of natural sexual difference and inequality. In addition, he opposes the social practice of individual similarity and equality, based on his ontological theory of natural individual difference and inequality—within races and between classes. Sexual similarity and equality are impossible and undesirable for the same reasons which make individual similarity and equality impossible and undesirable. Natural and social sexual equivalence, like natural and social individual equivalence, is primitive, unnatural, and dysfunctional.

Modern society is based on the distribution of specialized social functions according to differentiated natural structures. As opposed to feminism, this involves the hierarchical distribution of the two hierarchical human functions, familial and social, to women and men on the basis of sexually, hierarchically differentiated abilities. As opposed to racism, it involves the egalitarian *distribution* of the various hierarchical social functions to individual men according to individually, hierarchically differentiated abilities. As opposed to socialism, it involves the egalitarian distribution of the various *hierarchical* social functions to individual men based on individually, *hierarchically* differentiated abilities.

Men and women must be sorted not individually, but according to the principle of ascription, as two "races" or natural structures occupying two social functions and constituting a structural-functional caste system. Men must be sorted not ascriptively, but according to the principle of individual mobility, as a multitude of individuals or natural structures occupying a multitude of social functions and constituting a structural-functional system of equal opportunity. Once sorted, however, individual men constitute a social, economic hierarchy of functions, reflecting their natural, individual hierarchy of structures and thereby constituting a structural-functional system of class.

Feminism, like racism and socialism, divides society incorrectly. Feminism falsely confounds the two sexes into a single unified human species and falsely distinguishes among women as distinct, human individuals. Racism falsely confounds distinct human individuals into several unified races and falsely distinguishes among races as distinct, racial species. Socialism falsely confounds naturally distinct individuals and classes into a single unified human species in terms of the innate potential of diverse individual structures and the social value of diverse social functions, and it falsely distinguishes among individuals and classes as socially distinct political-economic groups in terms of power, wealth, and ownership of the means of production.

Because feminism, like socialism and racism, dissects the social body incorrectly—or worse, fails to conceive of society as a social body—it is an ideology that is as divisive and destructive as it is false. Feminism champions the rights of one component of the collective social subject, women, at the expense, and to the detriment or jeopardy, of the health and welfare of the collective social subject in its entirety: the collective consciousness, the social organism underlying the collective consciousness, and the institutional organs (marriage and the family) and individual cells (men) that compose the social organism.[35] Similarly, racism champions the rights of one putative race—for example, the French—and socialism champions the rights of one putative class—the working class—at the expense of the health and welfare of the collective social subject in its entirety and of its other component parts, notably Jews and capitalists.

Feminism, racism, and socialism are preempted in general by Durkheim's organicism and specifically by the way he constructs the structure of his social subject. Thus racism and socialism represent the theoretical cries and practical self-destruction of a sick and suffering social body, from which the scientific social biologist and the political social physician stand apart in clinical detachment, with correct social theory and therapeutic social practice. Similarly, feminism is "an unconscious movement" that "deceives itself when it formulates the details of its demands" (1980, 296).

Recuperation: Durkheim's "Feminism"

Durkheim has a dual relationship with feminism, just as he has a dual relationship with racism and socialism. He opposes racism, while denying that race exists and dismissing racism as simply false. He opposes socialism while redefining socialism and claiming to be a socialist. Similarly, Durkheim rejects feminism, yet he also redefines it and at least implicitly claims to be a feminist. Durkheim rejects "false" or unscientific feminism, defined as a quest for sexual equality. However, he supports true or "scientific" feminism, defined as a quest for sexual difference. Durkheim supports feminism in the sense that he supports the doctrine of separate but equal.

Durkheim counsels "woman" to "seek for equality in the functions which are commensurate with her nature." He identifies women's nature as "asocial" and the functions commensurate with that nature as "affective"—specifically, as familial functions. Durkheim thus advocates sexual equality, to the extent that sexual equality is defined as female specialization in the family. Furthermore, since women are located within the family, like cells in an organ, their interests are identical with the interests of the family. The well-being of women is contingent on the internal vitality of the family, and their social value is contingent on the relative position of the family within the social organism. Durkheim identifies the interests of women with the strength and sanctity of the traditional family.[36]

The health of the family is functional for women, and it depends on three factors. The family, like any social structure, organ or organism, requires solidarity: integration and regulation. According to Durkheim, the modern nuclear or "conjugal" family is integrated in two ways. Sexual specialization and interdependence create familial integration as the organic solidarity of conjugal society. Sexual stratification and hierarchy create familial integration as the patriarchal organization of conjugal society. And finally, according to Durkheim, the modern nuclear, conjugal family is regulated, and serves its function as sexual regulation, through indissoluble marriage.[37]

Durkheim identifies the interests of women with the interests of the family, and he identifies the interests of the family with the sexual division of labor, the patriarchal distribution of power, and the prohibition of divorce. Durkheim identifies feminism with familialism. Therefore his recuperation of feminism is in effect an inversion of feminism. By identifying women's interests with the traditional family, and thus with sexual specialization, sexual stratification, and indissoluble marriage, he identifies women's interests with the opposite of women's interests: with a sociosexual system of dual spheres and patriarchy. Durkheim thus encourages women to identify with, rather than oppose, men, the patriarchal family, and patriarchal society.

Women, who are outside society—nonhuman, asocial, and other than "individuals"—who are relegated to the nonsocial, nonhuman, animal sphere of biological reproduction, are nonetheless called upon to be "good citizens": to sacrifice their personal, egoistic, and anomic self-interests for the good of the social organism and collective consciousness from which they are excluded. More precisely, they are expected to identify their self-interests with the interests of men, "the family," and society—even though they are radically heterogeneous from men, forming a different and inferior species—because, tautologically, they and their domestic spheres are radically exterior to society.

Women should be integrated and regulated within the family and segregated from men and society as the substructural foundation of that all-male body; they are asked by Durkheim to meet with their bodies, by reproducing bodies, the functional imperatives of other bodies: men and society. Women, who are not social subjects, are to be subject to the sole social subjects, men, and to the collective male subject, society. Ironically, this exclusion from subjectivity, this subjection, is supposed to be "for their own good," in the interest of women, feminists, and feminism.

In a similar way, Durkheim's recuperation of socialism is in effect an inversion of socialism. By identifying workers' interests with "the division of labor in society," "modern society," "the social organism," the "collective consciousness," and "individualism" and thus with class specialization, class stratification, and private ownership of the means of production, he identifies workers' interests with the opposite of workers' interests: with a socioeconomic system of class and capitalism. Durkheim thus encourages workers to identify with, rather than oppose, capitalists, capitalist economic relations, and capitalist society.

Finally, Durkheim's antiracism is in effect an inversion of antiracism. By identifying the interests of subordinate cultures with the dominant culture and thus with cultural inequality, cultural hegemony, and assimilation, he identifies their interests with the opposite of their interests: with a sociocultural system of ethnocentrism and racism. Durkheim thus encourages subordinate cultures to identify with, rather than oppose, the dominant culture, ethnocentric cultural relations, and racist society.

Durkheim identifies feminism, racism, and socialism with ideology or false consciousness, which he opposes with his own Durkheimian structural-functional, organicist social "science." For Durkheim false consciousness is the analysis and critique, the description and proscription, the recognition and rejection of group-level, socially based, contingent, and detrimental inequality. Durkheim recognizes and supports human inequality, which he describes as individual-level, naturally based, necessary, and beneficial inequality. Based on this description, he prescribes identification of all "individuals" or cells (and even nonindividuals, i.e., women) with all other individual cells, with "society" or the social organism in its entirety, and with its constituent institutions or organs. Durkheimian social theory presents itself as feminism, socialism, and antiracism, but it is the very epitome of ideology or false consciousness from a feminist, Marxist, and/or multiculturalist perspective.

An Exceptional Instance: Sex versus Race and Class

Durkheim treats the theories and practices of racism, socialism, and feminism consistently. His general theoretical orientation, organicism, and his general political ideology, liberalism, require that he oppose them as false, divisive, and destructive. He treats the categories of race and class consistently. His general theoretical orientation, organicism, requires that he resolve them into the structural-functional categories of cells/individuals, organs/occupations, and organism/society. His general political ideology, liberalism, requires that he resolve them into the capitalist categories of individuals and occupations. At the same time an important contradiction, a decisive difference, in the way Durkheim treats the category of sex illuminates another dimension of his political ideology as well as another dimension of his social theory.

Durkheim eliminates the category of race from his social ontology, believing that in modern, complex society the hereditary transmission of simple, general abilities to groups—races—is replaced by the social transmission of complex, specific abilities to individuals. He eliminates the category of class[38] from his social ontology, believing that in modern, complex society the hereditary distribution of occupations to castes is replaced by equal opportunity and individual mobility. Natural processes are replaced by social processes, and natural groups are replaced by socialized individuals. Durkheim's liberalism is tempered by his organicism: he is oriented toward collectivism, statism, corporatism, social reform, and social determinism to a far greater extent than his laissez-faire contemporaries. Nonetheless, he is an unequivocal supporter of capitalism.

There is of course some ambiguity in Durkheim's work with respect to race and class. There is a latent tendency to a conservative theory of caste, manifest in conceptions of acquired characteristics at the individual, class, and social level. Thus Durkheim at least implies that individuals, classes, and societies may be arrayed in permanent hierarchies. In addition to stressing that modern skills are complex and socially acquired, he also maintains that individuals inherit differential occupational aptitudes, that there are innate individual skills and "natural hierarchies" of individual ability. Similarly, social classes inherit differential levels of general ability and can be trained only for specific tasks falling within those innate group parameters. Finally, societies possess differential levels of innate evolutionary capacity, and there are limits to universal modernity even within a unilinear evolutionary schema.

On the other hand, Durkheim's predominant tendency is to stress individualism, social acquisition, and equal opportunity as opposed to racialism, hereditary transmission, and caste. His work effectively opposes scientific racism and a "forced division of labor" and effectively promotes individual mobility. But Durkheim's theory of women is the glaring exception to his predominant liberalism. Durkheim is unambiguous and perfectly overt in his condemnation of women as inherently, essentially, universally, and eternally Other: different and inferior, biological rather than social, homogeneous rather than differentiated, primitive rather than modern, animal rather than human, outside society, beyond "*liberté, égalité, fraternité*," absent from the public sphere and exempt from liberal principles, nonexistent in a collective social being comprising and constituting modern, civilized, social, human "individuals."

Had Durkheim excluded any other human group from society, from socialization, from civilization, from modernity—from humanity—not only actually but also potentially—since for Durkheim women are unsocializable as well as unsocialized, perhaps it would not have taken a century for scholars to recognize and criticize his position. Had Durkheim unambiguously and overtly claimed that Europeans, or "primitives," or workers, or men could never be social and could never, therefore, aspire to morality, mentality, modernity—humanity—and should always, therefore, be relegated to a "separate sphere," excluded from "public" political, economic, and cultural life, perhaps his entire theoretical edifice would have been examined more carefully and more critically before the centenary of *The Division of Labor in Society*. It is hoped that the critical examination of the limits of neoliberal capitalist theory, as it relates to women, will form part of a critical examination of the limits of late capitalist reality as it relates to women and other modern castes.

Chapter 6

THE

CONTEMPORARY

MILIEU

- **The Structural Context**

Situating Durkheim in his structural context demonstrates that simply "reading Durkheim" is somewhat misleading. First, his decontextualized texts give the false impression that Durkheim's discourse and feminist discourse have nothing in common. On the contrary, Durkheim shared a belief in sexual difference and separate spheres with many of his feminist contemporaries and with some of ours. Second, his texts, taken out of context, give the false impression that his structural context was serene and silent, especially for women, and that women were all sitting quietly at home waiting for men to decide whether they should stay in their place or come outside into the public sphere. On the contrary, women were actively involved in extradomestic economic, political, and cultural life and were fighting hard to expand their rights in these arenas, as well as in the familial/domestic arena.

Reading other accounts of Durkheim's structural context demonstrates that his embrace of sexual difference and separate spheres was not in itself the deciding factor in classifying him as an antifeminist. Durkheim's structural setting was, like all social formations, extremely complex and was related in extremely complex ways to the discourses it produced. Durkheim's discourse was no exception: it was complex, and it was related in complex ways to his social environment and to other theoretical discourses. In particular, women were answering the woman question in practice, occupying the public "social" sphere en masse as paid laborers, political activists, and intellectuals. Durkheim's answer to the woman question in theory, that women should not *and could not* participate in society, placed him at odds with reality and virtually alone at the extreme end of the antifeminist continuum.

What about Durkheim's relationship to our milieu(s)? What about the relationship between his theories of capitalism and patriarchy and the realities of capitalism and patriarchy today? A century has elapsed since Durkheim's *The Division of Labor in Society* was published, and the value of his theory can be assessed retrospectively, "tested" by history. My judgment is that Durkheim was prescient in describing the intrinsic connection between capitalism and patriarchy while others predicted, some happily, some sadly, that capitalism would destroy patriarchy and all other caste relationships. Durkheim was also prescient in advocating and predicting the "social" reform of capitalism in the form of an expansion of state intervention in individual and economic activity.

At the same time, Durkheim was unjustifiably sanguine about the functionality of capitalist and patriarchal social structures and excessively optimistic about the promise and potential of social reform. Capitalism has been substantially reformed, and yet it continues to degenerate: it is more and more "dysfunctional," for more and more people, every day. On the other hand, the major reforms Durkheim both advocated and predicted—corporatism and collectivism—have not been effected. In addition, a caste system of ascription still exists: the majority of individuals are allocated positions in social-political-economic-cultural hierarchies on the basis of group identities—nationality, race, class, and sex—rather than individual abilities. Neither the pure capitalism of classic liberals nor the state capitalism of neoliberals has realized the claims made for it, in the short run or in the last instance.

Capitalism, even with a strong secular state, does not work. Poverty; unemployment; homelessness; colonialism; militarism; environmental, educational, and health-care crises; and crime are not ameliorated but aggravated as capitalism entrenches and expands its empire around the world. Patriarchy, whether hegemonic or contested by feminism, does not work. Family violence, divorce, and incest prevail despite the persistence of patriarchal structures and separate spheres. Women are treated differently and unequally as women, and they are not reverently worshiped for dutifully performing their domestic labor and child-care functions. At the same time, the mass entrance of women into the paid labor force has been accompanied by the feminization of poverty and the rise of virulent misogyny.

Conservative practices have not sanctified women, and liberal practices have not liberated them. Women are neither "different *but* equal," nor similar *and* equal, in relation to men. They share oppression with men under the structured inequality and human misery of capitalism, racism, and colonialism. In addition, they are subject to specific oppression because of their biological characteristics. Women are victimized, as women, by pornographic rape, pornographic femicide, pornographic culture, and pornography. As women they suffer sexual harassment, the glass ceiling, national and international dual labor markets, lower pay, a double day, single parenthood, unemployment, underemployment, homelessness, and the welfare system. The persistence of separate spheres, coupled with the persistence of privatized domestic labor and child care, renders women economically dependent on men or the welfare state or forces them to work a second shift.

Women, as women, are subject to patriarchal structures and sexist, misogynist cultures. This is true of all women, in all places: partnered women and single women; women with children, women without children; women who are waged workers, women who are homemakers, and "superwomen" who are both; women who are in the paid labor force by choice or necessity and women who are out of the paid labor force by choice or necessity; femisexual women, bisexual women, and heterosexual women; women in dominant races/cultures, women in subordinate races/cultures; women in industrial colonialist societies and women in underdeveloped colonized societies.

It is possible that there is more diversity among women in the contemporary world, although the image of greater uniformity in other eras is probably somewhat illusory. It is certain that the combined existence of patriarchy and feminist opposition to patriarchy have to this point delivered women up to the worst of both worlds. It is also certain that the combined existence of patriarchy with capitalism, racism, and colonialism has ravaged women in a specifically savage way. And it is certain that women are beset by the same problems that plagued them in Durkheim's time, in addition to the problems that are unique to the twentieth century.

As Susan Faludi (1991) has powerfully argued, feminist progress has been a slow, modest, arduous process of "one step forward, one step back"; yet feminist gains are exaggerated and frequently blamed for the problems of men, women, children, and society. A comparison of the contemporary structural milieu with

Durkheim's structural milieu, one that recognizes the existence of feminist theory and practice in the late nineteenth century as well as the existence of patriarchal theory and practice in the late twentieth century, produces a sense of "plus ça change, plus elle reste la même."

The Discursive Context

Durkheim's sexual discourse was both more compatible with feminist discourses in Third Republic France and less compatible with them than we might imagine by looking at it in abstraction from his discursive context. But what about the relationship between Durkheim's discourse and contemporary discourses on women and society? Clearly the notion that women are asocial, incapable of achieving modern, human status as mental and moral beings, is external to all official, recognized theoretical problematics, although it is intrinsic to the pornographic theorization of women. But what about sexual difference and separate spheres? Are these compatible with, or even central to, "feminism"? What is feminism anyway? Is feminism a singular or a plural theory and practice? Is there one "feminism," or are there multiple "feminisms"? What are the relationships between feminisms and other social theories such as liberalism and Marxism?

Feminism is perhaps singular *and* plural: there may be theoretical and practical convergence as well as theoretical and practical divergence on the woman question, at the end of the twentieth century as at the end of the nineteenth, and among partisans of various theoretical and practical answers to "the social question." In relation to "political" discourse on society Durkheim was prescient, anticipating the liberal rationale for reformist extension of individual rights to more individuals and the neoliberal rationale for reformist extension of state intervention to more activities. In relation to "apodictic" discourse on society he was also prescient, anticipating the rigorous social determinism or sociologism that came to dominate structuralism and poststructuralism alike.[1]

At the same time, Durkheim was politically and ideologically retrograde, demurring from the universal extension of individual rights and the feminist, multiculturalist, internationalist, socialist transformation of patriarchy, racism, imperialism, and capitalism. Durkheim was also apodictically and scientifically retrograde, articulating social theories based on organicism, evolutionism, structural functionalism, and positivism, doctrines that are currently being displaced and transcended both from the perspective of scientism, as unscientific, and from the perspective of antiscientism, as symptomatically scientific.

The dominant political and theoretical positions that prevail today in advanced industrial societies are various forms of liberalism, generally combined with various conservative exceptions with respect to race, class, sex, and/or nation. However, liberal theory and "modern" practice are increasingly unsatisfactory and unsatisfying, in the old modern societies as well as in their "modernizing" and "developing" colonies. With respect to women, the dominant ideologies are particularly unsatisfactory and unsatisfying, since liberalism does not suffice as a liberational ideology for women, and while it is insufficient in itself, it is powerfully undermined by pervasive and resurgent conservatism on the woman question. Liberalism is nonetheless the dominant popular form of feminism: liberals are still attempting to destroy patriarchy by realizing the potential of capitalism. The totalizing ideological control of late capitalism does not permit ideological diversity outside the polarities: classic liberalism/neoliberalism and inconsistent liberalism/consistent liberalism.

The dominant apodictic/theoretical positions are schismatic, divided into an infinity of theoretical factions and variants of factions. Feminist theory is attempting both to critically appropriate ontologies and epistemologies from other social theories and to autonomously develop its own specific ontologies and epistemologies. It is attempting to navigate the treacherous waters of theoretical Marxisms, symbolic interactionisms, structuralisms, poststructuralisms, post-poststructuralisms, neofunctionalisms, neosocial biologisms, multiculturalisms, deconstructionisms, postmodernisms, antipostmodernisms, etcetera ad infinitum while it is itself internally differentiated into a multiplicity of feminisms, related in a multiplicity of ways to other theoretical problematics.

Feminist theory is one of the most vibrant and dynamic forms of social theory today, and there are constant developments and contentious debates within it. One concerns its continuous expansion to be ever more inclusive and representative of diversity and difference among women—differences of class, race, nationality, sexuality—and ever more expository and critical of structures and cultures of inequality. Although popular feminism remains committed to liberalism/capitalism, to the extent that critiques of and alternatives to this position and this system are excluded from popular discourse, theoretical feminism has moved beyond liberalism. First it adopted a primary focus on patriarchy to become radical feminism; then it encompassed Marxism to become socialist feminism; and finally it has embraced theoretical opposition to racism and imperialism to become multicultural feminism.

A second development/debate within feminist theory is a return to (or a continued insistence on) sexual difference and separate spheres. This renewal resonates with Karen Offen's description of continental European feminism, which she calls "relational" or "familial" feminism, with cultural feminism, and with radical feminism. Sexual difference, or essentialism, and separate spheres, or separatism, are strong tendencies within French feminism, which comes as no surprise given Offen's analysis of Europe in general and France in particular, in which sexual essentialism and sexual separatism exist at the theoretical inter-section of the very conservative and the very radical. Sexual difference/essence and sexual spheres/separation theories are also closely aligned with poststruc-turalist ontology and epistemology, which also comes as no surprise, given the Francocentric nature of both movements.[2]

Renewed interest in theories of sexual difference, conservative and radical, is perhaps understandable given the overwhelming difficulty of, and opposition to, feminism, defined as sexual freedom, sexual equality, sexual androgyny, sexual integration, full employment for both sexes, socialized domestic labor and child care—even as de facto equal opportunity and individual mobility for women. Given this difficulty and this opposition, along with the chronic col-lapse, crisis, and vicissitudes of global capitalism, a retreat to dual spheres may seem necessary and/or desirable, and thus theories of sexual difference would have a new appeal in describing the eternal, and prescribing the inevitable, differential structures and specialized functions of women versus men. At the same time, "different" feminisms continue to hold out significantly different models and ideals, describing structural sexual similarity and prescribing func-tional sexual resemblance.

Given the plethoric disarray of contemporary feminist theory and practice, and given Durkheim's unequivocal antifeminism, what can or should be the relationship between feminist theory and Durkheimian theory? Does Dur-kheim's theoretical discourse have anything of value to offer feminist theoretical discourse? I think there are five conceivable ways feminist theory could crit-ically appropriate Durkheimian theory.

First, Durkheim's work on the differential effects of marriage and divorce on men and women, as demonstrated by their differential suicide rates, suggests theoretical and empirical approaches to the divergent conditions and hos-tilities of interest that divide the sexes. Specifically, Durkheim's work in *Suicide* offers the promise of a theory of female fatalism as the converse of male anomie.[3] In other words, Durkheim comes close to a critical rejection of his own theory of organic social unity, as he comes close to a sociological theory of conflictual sexual difference.

Second, more generally, Durkheim's social determinism and sociologism could be used—without exception, without advocacy, without resignation, fa-talism, reification, or hypostatization—to understand the social nature of sexual difference. Critical feminist descriptions of the social structure of patriarchy and its effects could complement critical Marxist descriptions of capitalism and critical multiculturalist descriptions of racism and colonialism. Critical feminist theories of patriarchy could also complement critical feminist practices of transforming patriarchy. Finally, critical feminist research and theory about patriarchy can serve as a corrective to positivist patriarchal research and theory about patriarchy. In *A Sociology of Women,* for example, Jane C. Ollenburger and Helen A. Moore (1992) suggest something along these lines when they propose improving the relationship between women's studies and the social sciences.

Third, Durkheim's scientific theory of social determinism could be appropriated by feminism as an alternative to the "scientific" theory of individualism. The rigorous application of social determinism, within a feminist framework, to epistemological and ontological problems, could help to break down theoretical barriers, break up theoretical logjams, and move beyond theoretical dead ends caused by the totalizing, pervasive, and tenacious liberal ideology of bourgeois capitalist, patriarchal hegemony. Individualism obscures social structural processes, obfuscates social structural inequalities, occludes social structural critique, and obstructs social structural change. Individualism not only misleads proletarian individuals about their structural relations of exploitation and dependence vis-à-vis capitalist individuals, it also misleads female "individuals" about their structural relations as economic, political, and cultural nonentities, segregated from the public sphere and social contracts of genuine, universal, universally male "individuals."

In addition, a rigorous critical application of social determinism without exception to all social groups, including races, classes, sexes, and nations, could serve as a corrective to racism, classism, sexism, nationalism, and imperialism. Durkheim, along with Marx, provided a foundation for multiculturalism, structuralism, and poststructuralism through his theoretical social determinism, in which individuals and groups are viewed as products, not producers, of their specific social positions within specific social structures. When races, classes, sexes, and nations are viewed as distinct *cultures,* existing in determinate relations within distinct *structures,* then the questions of cause, effect, and intervention can be posed within a new problematic, where inequality is social and contingent, not natural and necessary.

A fourth aspect of Durkheimian theory with potential value for feminist theory and practice would be Durkheim's neoliberal critique of the political practice of individualism manifest in laissez-faire capitalism. Durkheim's recommendations for the social reform of capitalism—as the integration and regulation of economics and individuals at the societal and occupational levels through a strong state, a secular education system, and occupational organizations—was ahead of its time and is still far from being realized. His promotion of extraindividual and extraeconomic social processes and exigencies was a collectivist and moralist orientation that could be invoked today for the reform of late, state capitalism. In *Feminism without Illusions,* for example, Elizabeth Fox-Genovese (1991) uses a Durkheimian framework to critique an individualistic social order, and classic liberal, individualistic feminism, from the standpoint of social and collective needs and interests.

Finally, feminists could potentially use Durkheim to examine real relationships among real social structures—capitalism, patriarchy, racialism, and colonialism—and among real social groups—classes, sexes, races, and nations. This complex nexus can be understood generally, as the relationships between ostensible systems of competitive individual mobility and equal opportunity, and actual systems of caste. Durkheim recognized these relationships and articulated them, sometimes critically, sometimes positively, often ambiguously—sometimes consciously, sometimes unconsciously, often semiconsciously. Durkheim the social draftsman recorded the conceptualization that social architects held of the new social order they were constructing (and by which they were being constructed). More to the point, feminists could use Durkheim's theory as a model of theoretical relationships, for example, the "ideological" constellations of classic liberalism, neoliberalism, and conservatism; the "scientific" constellations of organicism, structural functionalism, and positivism; and the relationships between Durkheimian, hegemonic social theory and genuinely alternative theoretical problematics.

Feminism *could* critically appropriate Durkheimian theory as possibly useful to its theory and practice. However, the question remains: *Should* feminism return to Durkheim for theoretical or practical insight into the "structures and functions" of patriarchy and its relations with other social structures? Or to pose the question in a Durkheimian way: Is it *necessary* or *beneficial* to perform a feminist sublation of Durkheim's naturalistic descriptions and defenses of the marriage of capitalism and patriarchy? In a quest for anti-individualistic theories of social structures and social determinism, is it necessary or beneficial to appropriate structural functional social determinism? In a quest for scientific epistemologies to comprehend and transform social structural and cultural reality, is it necessary or beneficial to appropriate positivistic epistemologies? In a quest for anti-individualistic social practices of "socialism" and collectivism, is it necessary or beneficial to appropriate organicist "socialism" and collectivism?

It seems to me that feminist scholarship is caught between the Scylla and Charybdis of structural functionalism and poststructuralism, in a false dichotomy constructed by poststructuralism.[4] Poststructuralism rejects the form and content of structural functionalism, the organicist ontologies and positivist epistemologies that coalesce in naturalistic hypostatizations of "reality"—that is, the "modern" sciences of "modern" structures, including patriarchy, capitalism, racialism, and imperialism. Because of the apparently radical nature of poststructuralism, its militant opposition to conservative theories and oppressive realities, it is seductive to critical theorists and transformative activists— feminists, Marxists, multiculturalists.

Poststructuralism, with all its variants—deconstruction, postmodernism, post-Marxism, postfeminism, and so on—marks the point at which ultraradical theory dovetails with ultraconservative theory. While poststructuralism is celebrating the end of science in theory and the end of structures in reality, neostructural functionalism is proclaiming "the end of ideology," "the end of history," "the death of Marxism," "the death of communism," and the advent of "postindustrial society."[5] Poststructuralism focuses on the way scientific theory has created the illusion of structural reality. It conflates critical scientific theory with conservative scientific theory as the "modern" episteme, socialist structural reality with capitalist structural reality as the "modern" ontology, which—social structure—either never existed or no longer exists.

Along with its epistemological and ontological conflations, which I think are unfounded, poststructuralism tends to conflate epistemology and ontology (as "discourse," "objects," "text," or "difference") and to privilege epistemology or theory at the expense of ontology or "reality." Viewing social structures primarily as figments of the sociological imagination, poststructuralism criticizes scientific theory and, by design or by default, deflects attention from, or denies, structural reality. It is my contention, and that of other "post-poststructuralists,"[6] that social problems are ontological rather than epistemological—problems of reality, not of theory. Further, I contend that to "solve" social problems in theory, and not in reality—to imply that oppressive social structures do not exist except as the artifacts of an outmoded modern Western episteme or that oppression is an epistemological rather than an ontological problem—is to take a conservative stance, the stance of an ostrich, with respect to "real" social problems, their "real" social structural existences, and their "real" social structural solutions.

To put it another way, social problems are not caused by the "conservatism" of critical social theories like Marxism and feminism, with their models of deleterious social structures and dichotomous structural hierarchies. Rather, social problems are caused by the only too real structures and hierarchies that critical theories describe as realities, critique as deleterious realities, and strive to transform as contingent realities. The "old" modern critical theories are not conservative; they cannot be conflated with the "old" modern conservative theories, which describe social structures as realities, support them as beneficial, and seek to conserve them as necessary. Conservative theories are not declaring themselves irrelevant or their realities nonexistent; the former actively contribute to the preservation and prosperity of the latter.[7]

It seems premature, then, to move beyond modern theories of reality when modern structures of reality are still in existence. Neither the "old" conservative defenses nor the "old" critical attacks can be surpassed or become outmoded as long as the "old" social structures they "refer" to are neither surpassed nor outmoded—despite the consumptionist fetish for the "obsolescence" and "novelty" of theoretical commodities. It seems unreasonable to take the postmodern turn beyond critical social science in theory when we are in no meaningful sense beyond capitalism, patriarchy, racism, or imperialism in reality. It seems unreasonable to become post-Marxist in a capitalist (not a postcapitalist or postliberal) world, postfeminist in a patriarchal (not a postpatriarchal or post-sexist) world, poststructuralist in a structural (not a poststructural or postscientific) world. The absurdity of this theoretical wishful thinking can perhaps be highlighted by extending it ad absurdam: surely no one will suggest that we are living in a postracist world and can entertain postantiracist theories, or that we are living in a postimperialist world and can entertain postanti-imperialist theories. Will multiculturalism ever be obsolete?

Feminists and other critical theorists and practitioners are confronted with an apparent choice between structural functionalism and positivism, on the one hand, and poststructuralism and skepticism on the other. Feminism concerned with studying social structures in scientific ways seems to have only one alternative: the reifying realism and hypostatizing determinism of Durkheimian structural functionalism. Positivistic structural functionalism is an optimistic ontoepistemological theory for adherents of the ontoepistemological status quo, but a fatalistic and fatal theory for its critics. Positivistic structural functionalism, with its liberal counterpart in political-economic ideology, is unable to account for social problems except to attribute them to social structural absences and to individual deviations and deficiencies. It insists that social structures exist and are intelligible. But it insists on positive (necessary, beneficial, adaptive, evolutionary) structures and on positive (unproblematic, untheoretical, positing, approbative, pro-) knowledge.

Feminism concerned with affirming the possibilities of egalitarian, liberational social practice and social change also seems to have only one alternative: the relativizing nominalism and leveling indeterminacy of post-Durkheimian poststructuralism. Poststructuralism is a satisfying and useful theory for critics of the epistemological status quo but a frustrating and futile theory for critics of the ontological status quo. Relativistic poststructuralism, with its liberal counterpart in political-economic ideology, is unable to account for social problems except to attribute them to social structural presences, in theory and (therefore) in reality. It insists that social structures do not exist and are (therefore) unintelligible. And it insists on negative (unnecessary, detrimental, oppressive, nonexistent) structures and negative (relativistic and illusory or negating and critical, anti-) knowledge.

Positivistic structural functionalism and relativistic poststructuralism appear to be exclusive and mutually exclusive diametrically oppositional theories. However, this is a false dichotomy, for several reasons. First, they appear as opposites only within a general liberal, humanistic problematic. That is, they are both theories that pose the entities "individuals" and "social structures" as oppositional categories.

Structural functionalism and its neoliberal counterpart maintain that there is/should be a balance or equilibrium between social structural and individual imperatives. Social structures govern individuals in their own interest, and/or individuals choose their social structures through consensus, and/or individuals voluntarily accept social structures in conscious obedience to internalized "norms," and/or there is an asocial sphere of individual/economic contracts that operates as a "free zone" parallel to a social sphere of collective/social contracts that operates as a regulated zone. Structural functionalism further maintains that social, categorical inequalities merely reflect natural, individual inequalities and that they are "functional" provided conditions of equal opportunity apply.

Poststructuralism and its radical liberal counterpart[8] maintain that there is an absolute antagonism between social structural and individual imperatives, and that there is a zero-sum game between social determinism and individual freedom. Poststructuralism and radical liberalism alike lapse into the contradiction of declaring all human individuals naturally, essentially, and absolutely free while decrying the unnatural, contingent, but absolute unfreedom suffered by individuals trapped in (or believing themselves trapped in) social structures.[9]

The only practical options open to those who would liberate natural human individuals from artificial social structures are individual resistance and withdrawal from social structures, and/or collective destruction of social structures, and/or pessimistic resignation in the face of universal totalitarian social structures (the mainstream Frankfurt School "solution"). Or else they might liberate natural human individuals from artificial social structures "in theory"—taking the position that social structures are theoretical constructions, created by science (realism), maintained by ideology (reification), and sustained by philosophy (the metaphysics of presence) and that therefore they can be theoretically deconstructed—destroyed by antiscience, philosophical skepticism, relativism, nominalism, negation, negative dialectics, criticism.[10]

Poststructuralism castigates all other social theories as "modern," hence as "conservative," "grand narrative," "Western," "metaphysical." Poststructuralism thus poses as the only critical, radical, newer, and better social theory. But the backlash against poststructuralism has already begun. The wry predictions of "post-poststructuralism" that greeted the coining of "poststructuralism" have been realized. I would like to intervene and suggest a way out of this problem of nomenclature and, more important, a way out of the current theoretical impasse of feminism and other critical praxis.

With respect to nomenclature, I believe that the "posts" are actually "antis" and that antistructuralism, anti-Marxism, antifeminism, antideterminism, antimodernism, antiscientism, etc., not only antedate but coexist with and predate their epistemological and ontological opposites. The posts "oppose" their opponents in new and more sophisticated ways and for new and better reasons. Yet the conflict is an enduring one, and in some sense the "posts" are returning to an old position on an old terrain and ironically capitalizing on an old theme: the alleged superiority of the new to the old, the later to the earlier, that is, the theoretical commodity fetish: "post" sounds superior to "pre" and more recondite than "anti."

Similarly, "post-poststructuralism" can be seen as a return to, a defense of, an advocacy of some of the ontological and epistemological principles of structuralism—although it is an advocacy that takes into account the critiques and positions of poststructuralism as well as the differentiation among various meanings and practices of "structuralism": it is a critical and sublative advocacy of a particular form of structuralism. To simplify the "name" of this theoretical problematic without losing the complexity of its relation to other forms of structuralism and to post- or antistructuralism, I call this problematic "critical structuralism."[11]

In some ways feminism is in a quandary, caught with other critical praxes in a dilemma between structural functionalism's acceptance of, and complicity with, extant social structures, hierarchies, castes, and categories and poststructuralism's denial of the ontological existence, the epistemological "truth" of social structures, hierarchies, classes, and categories. Critical structuralism offers a way out of this dilemma as well as a way out of the paradoxes of various forms of liberalism. Critical structuralism asks the "modern" theoretical question: Are there natural, internal, structural differences and inequalities between and among nations, races, classes, cultures, sexes, and sexualities to justify their different and unequal social positions and relations? If not, why are most (but not all) of them subordinate, poor, oppressed, exploited, endangered?

The conservative answer is that there are qualitative differences among groups of people, which are and should be expressed in intrasocial and international structures of caste. Critical structuralism's preliminary answer is that destructive and dysfunctional but mutable social structures—patriarchy, capitalism, racialism, imperialism—condemn the majority of human beings to gratuitous misery and suffering. The liberal answer is equivocal. Liberalism denies that there are systematic natural differences and inequalities among individuals at the group level, to make a case for equal opportunity and individual mobility and against caste systems of ascription. But liberalism maintains that there are natural differences and inequalities among individuals; that is, at the individual level.

Critical structuralism interrogates the liberal position: *Are* there natural, internal, structural differences and inequalities between and among *individuals* to justify their different and unequal social positions and relations? If not, why are most (but not all) of them subordinate, poor, oppressed, exploited, endangered? Unlike liberalism, critical structuralism answers no to this question as well, evoking some of the egalitarian possibilities of an absolute social determinism. If individuals are totally socially constituted, there can be no question of innate, natural, given, presocial differences and inequalities at *any* level.

The follow-up to this question and answer homes in on the mechanisms of distribution within liberal, stratified social structures: the differential and unequal *social* distribution of abilities to individuals, and social distribution of individuals to positions: Is there truly equal opportunity and individual mobility operating to align (putative) individual, structural differences and inequalities with social, functional differences and inequalities? If not, how *are* individuals and positions aligned, allocated, and distributed? Liberalism answers that perpetual, hereditary, group-level unequal opportunity does not exist, or that it exists as a survival of the feudal system of ascription, as an anomaly that can and will be corrected within and by capitalism.

Critical structuralism answers that capitalism is intrinsically and inextricably bound up with caste systems of ascription, as well as with patriarchy, racialism, and imperialism, and that under capitalism possession and dispossession, power and powerlessness, voice and voicelessness, freedom and subjection, dependence and independence will always be unequal and will always be perpetuated, inherited, acquired, ascriptively, on the basis of group-level characteristics—class, sex, race, and nationality.

Finally, critical structuralism asks this question of all social theories: Are social differences and inequalities justified regardless of the distribution mechanism employed? Can the deployment of individuals to positions, or rather the deployment of positions itself, be egalitarian, in line with the egalitarian potentialities, needs, and rights of all individuals, according to equity and justice rather than "efficiency" or "functionality"? Pursued to its logical extreme, this question ends up as the question of egalitarianism as a principle in its own right: Is egalitarianism of outcomes a reasonable social principle *regardless* of the natures of diverse individuals and groups, their potential differences and inequalities in ability, and regardless of the natures of diverse social functions, their potential differences and inequalities in social utility?

Critical structuralism involves theories of social ontology, methods of social analysis, mechanisms of social transformation, and ideals of social potential. It offers a third, alternative, approach for feminism and other critical activities to acknowledge structures, cultures, and practices of inequality without naturalizing social structures or simplifying social sciences. It offers a perspective on inequality and difference, according to which socialization is everything, individual and group "natures" nothing, where social processes and outcomes are actually differential and hierarchical but potentially egalitarian and liberating.

Critical structuralism is opposed to essentialism—the old conservative essentialism in which subordinate individuals and groups are seen as essentially different and inferior, or the new radical essentialism in which subordinate individuals and groups are seen as essentially different and equal or superior. Critical structuralism judges, evaluates, and discriminates among structures and cultures, not individuals and groups. In a similar vein, critical structuralism views various structures and cultures of inequality as inextricably interrelated. Therefore critical structuralism seeks an interrelationship among critical theories and transformative practices directed at structures, cultures, and practices of inequality.

Critical structuralism seeks, for example, to connect and reconnect feminism, Marxism, and multiculturalism, to mediate and attenuate the mutual ignorance and suspicion among them.[12] This aim is shared with cultural studies, and critical structuralism forms one of two tendencies central to cultural studies.[13] Critical structuralism shares with cultural studies an interdisciplinary, theoretically informed, critical, and activist stance in relation to multiple and interrelated structures of inequality, which draws upon and contributes to feminism, Marxism, and multiculturalism. In this sense it is also closely related to multicultural feminism and global feminism—which incorporate Marxist critiques of capitalism and classism, multiculturalist critiques of cultural and national imperialism, internal and external colonialism, racism, ethnocentrism, and nationalism, with a feminist critique of patriarchy and heterosexism, sexism, misogyny, and homophobia.[14]

Critical structuralism constitutes a theory and practice that combines traditional Marxist attention to economics with neo-Marxist attention to power/politics and culture/ideology/knowledge. It combines "materialist" attention to social structures with "idealist" attention to discourses as well as structuralist/poststructuralist attention to the inextricability of structure and discourse. And it unites a "macro" attention to individuals and interactions as socially determined with a "micro" attention to social structures as contingent and mutable, as well to subjective experience.

Critical structuralism combines structuralist attention to the reality and intelligibility of social structures with critical attention to the contradictions, conflicts, and dysfunctional and destructive effects of social structures. Finally, it conjoins a "negative" pessimistic attitude about the deleterious and powerful effects of specific structures of inequality with a "positive" optimistic view about the possibility of destroying destructive social structures and constructing constructive social structures. Critical structuralism is, in an understated word, complex!

I think it is especially important for feminism to explore the relationships among structural functionalism, critical structuralism, and poststructuralism because I believe, with Angela Davis, that feminism is the current vanguard of critical social theory and transformative social practice. Feminism has already grown and developed to encompass sexual, economic, racial, and national inequality in economic, political, and cultural spheres. It is already challenging patriarchy, sexism, and misogyny locally and globally, as well as militarism, poverty, racism, environmental destruction, war, and imperialism. Perhaps we can appropriate Kingsley Davis's (1959) formulation that structural functionalism is not a particular theory or method within sociology but *is* sociology: feminism is not a particular theory or method within critical structuralism, it *is* critical structuralism.

Feminism can reject Durkheimian social determinism as naturalist, functionalist, and conservative and Durkheimian/neoliberal collectivism as patriarchal, capitalist, and latently racist and imperialist. At the same time, it can reject classic liberalism and individualism as blind to social structural determinism and collective, universal, and equal rights, needs, and objectives. Finally, feminism can reject poststructuralism as opposing critical appropriation of structuralist insights and scientific practices, of prematurely and philosophically eliminating the necessity and possibility of scientific knowledge and the necessity and possibility of structural transformation. Feminism can embrace what Richard Johnson (1986/87) calls "post-post-structuralism," "radical structuralism," or "radical constructivism"—what Patrick Brantlinger (1990) identifies as part of the "cultural studies" project—and what I call, for clarity and distinction, critical structuralism.

Feminism, aligned with critical structuralism, can ask: Are men and women of the same human race and species and therefore ultimately subject to equal and similar social participation and treatment? Or are they fundamentally different, of different races or species, and therefore subject to different and unequal social participation and treatment? My answer, from a feminist/critical structuralist position, is that women and men are part of the same human species or race, but they belong to different and unequal *cultures.* Thus our first objective should be to equalize the social participation and treatment of the two cultures—masculine and feminine. Our second objective should be to destroy them.[15]

Conclusion

The comparison of Durkheim's milieu with our own can be troubling. Comparing his "material" or "real" environment with ours can lead to pessimism and relativism. The same social structures that were consolidated at the end of the nineteenth century—patriarchy; capitalism; internal, interracial colonialism; external, international imperialism—appear so entrenched, tenacious, and adaptive at the end of the twentieth century that it is tempting to lapse into fatalistic resignation and nihilistic despair or to revive existential angst. The social conflicts and social problems that are attendant on these social structures seem so persistent as to be "natural": they seem to provide unfortunate proof of positivist presuppositions about the universal and eternal property of social facts.

Transnational and transhistorical comparison of alternative social systems seems to undermine idealistic optimism and to reinforce cynical and pragmatic pessimism. All social systems appear equally beneficial or, conversely, equally detrimental. All appear equally dynamic on the surface, equally static at their foundations. Fundamental social change and progressive social change seem impossible. Weber's "iron cage" of bureaucratic, rationalized industrial capitalism merges with Durkheim's "modern," "specialized" industrial capitalism as the ultimate stage of social evolution and with Marx's prediction of a penultimate stage of polarized and immiserating global capitalism.

Many fin-de-siècle ontologies imply that there is no dichotomous difference, or at least no hierarchical order, between socialist and capitalist socioeconomic systems, between feminist and patriarchal sex-gender systems, or between workers and capitalists, women and men, dominant and subordinate cultures, within these systems. Every social structure and every social group—in fact, every historical moment and every unique being—is leveled into mere "difference," which, universally applied, levels all social "reality" into similarity. Social criticism and social change no longer refer to any radically "other" social arrangements, fulfilling the worst-case scenario of the Frankfurt school's critical theory. Capitalism and patriarchy have been around so long they have come back into fashion, and social "alternatives" are alternative forms of capitalism and patriarchy.

Grassroots social protest has been effectively obstructed and silenced as social victimization, at the national and international level, is inversely related to economic wealth, political power, and cultural "voice." Middle-class social protest has been effectively eviscerated and channeled into the false dichotomies of separate sexual spheres or sexual assimilation, and laissez-faire capitalism or state capitalism. The impulse to transform society has *at best* been shattered, been eroded, or transformed itself into the impulse to reform society. At worst, "relative deprivation" has turned objectively "vertical" struggles against a dominant system, class, sex, culture, or nation into "horizontal" struggles against other subordinate groups: classism, racism, misogyny, ethnocentrism, nationalism, and xenophobia, as well as callousness toward human suffering, seem endemic to "modernity."[16]

Comparing the intellectual or discursive dimension of Durkheim's environment with ours is similarly troubling and can equally lead to pessimism and relativism. The same intellectual conflicts, the same discursive debates, have been waged and discussed within Eurocentric culture for three centuries. Clearly, contradictory discursive structures, like contradictory social structures, seem enduring if not eternal. From a historical perspective, genuine change or progress in social discourse seems as chimerical as genuine change or progress in social reality. In retrospect, all discourse seems equally true or, conversely, equally false. There appears to be an "eternal return" at the cultural as well as the structural level of social life.

Looking at Durkheim's theoretical context is actually looking at his intellectual context out of context, and it is profoundly disquieting to scrutinize the earnest, ardent truth claims of other times and other places in all their stark absurdity. The arguments of others seem preposterous, and therefore a comparative approach is conducive to some extreme epistemological reactions. Familiarity with other theoretical frameworks can breed contempt for the will to knowledge in general. Relativism results from the assumption that our own discourse would appear as ludicrous in other contexts as the discourse of other contexts appears to us. All discourse is leveled into ideology, where the only apodictic distinctions are among various forms of sophistry, pretense, illusion, and deception.

A contrasting reaction to the now facile attempts of our intellectual antecedents to convince themselves and others that the truth was at hand, is the leveling of all discourse into truth. This is the approach taken by Durkheim, who felt that the subject of knowledge is the collective, social subject, which can never be wrong—it can only produce more or less accurate models of reality. The first attempts at knowledge are necessarily crude and rough, but over time they become refined, toward an ultimate Hegelian telos of total, universal self-knowledge by the collective subject of its objectified, universal self. This is the predominant empirical, epistemological episteme, the cumulative theory of knowledge, that Althusser describes pejoratively as "the history of knowledge."

Whether all "knowledge" is seen as more or less false (relativism) or as more or less true (positivism), all knowledge is reduced to a unity, a unity of infinite difference: the infinite difference of incremental advancement toward truth, or the infinite difference of heterogeneous posturing by heterogeneous impostors. Historical archaeology and grammatological deconstruction of previous discursive practices and discourses has most recently culminated in skepticism. Reading Bell and Offen's two-volume collection of discourses on the woman question tends to culminate in the same attitude. The discursive "overdetermination"—the wide diversity of "arguments" intended to prove a single point or justify a single practice, the complete similarity of "arguments" intended to prove disparate points or justify disparate practices—is stupefying.

Whether the reaction to historical discourse is one of skepticism in relation to all "science," "knowledge," and "truth" or one of condescending tolerance in relation to all "ideology," "falsehood," and "primitive classification," the result is the same. The realm of theory is a monolithic one, an undifferentiated, heterogeneous homogeneity of relativity. Many fin-de-siècle epistemologies imply that there is no dichotomous difference, or at least no hierarchical order, between socialist and capitalist theories, between feminist and patriarchal theories, between multicultural and ethnocentric theories, or between various contending positions within these theoretical systems. Every theoretical structure and faction, every theoretical moment and ideational element, is leveled into mere "difference," which, universally applied, levels all social theory into similarity.

With respect to feminism, this "postmodern" "chaos" is daunting, as is the historical order. Patriarchal social structures seem intact and vital, coexisting in a perplexing way with "postfeminism." Patriarchal theory seems intact and vital, coexisting curiously with the deconstructionist demurral to distinguish between ideology and science. The structural and theoretical separate spheres and sexual essentialism of traditional patriarchy seem intact and vital, coexisting comfortably with "feminist" (postfeminist?) versions of separate spheres and sexual essentialism. In the face of contemporary theory and reality, it becomes increasingly difficult, a difficulty engendered by the modern conservatives as well as by the postmodern radicals, to focus on women as a distinct and subordinate sociocultural group and to scientifically analyze the causes of, and solutions to, their distinctively sexual oppression. Feminists face the false dichotomy of patriarchal structures and structural functionalist theory versus postfeminist practices and poststructuralist theory.

I simply propose an alternative, third, position as a way out of this ontological and epistemological dilemma. It is a rejection of patriarchal structures and structural functionalist theory, but it stops short of postfeminist practices and poststructuralist theory. I call this critical social theory critical structuralism to denote that it acknowledges extant social structures, but from a critical perspective, according to which they can and should be transformed through critical social practice. From the standpoint of critical structuralism, "modern" social structures have survived the postmodernist new wave of utopianism, and "modern" social theories have survived the poststructuralist new wave of skepticism.

The persistence of patriarchy entails the persistence of the feminist alternative in theory and practice. The persistence of capitalism entails the persistence of the socialist alternative, in theory and practice. The persistence of colonialism entails the persistence of the multiculturalist alternative in theory and practice. There is, within this modern world, what Althusser would call an "eternal" struggle, not between modernism and "postmodernism" or between structural functionalism and poststructuralism, but between sexual, economic, cultural, and international egalitarianism, which criticizes theories, practices, structures, and sciences of inequality, and these same inegalitarian theories, practices, structures, and sciences.

There are real, structural dichotomies and hierarchies between capitalists and workers, men and women, dominant cultures and subordinate cultures, colonizers and colonials. Therefore there are theoretical and practical dichotomies and hierarchies, albeit extremely complicated, complex dichotomies and hierarchies, between science and ideology, structuralism and individualism, materialism and idealism, feminism and sexism, Marxism and liberalism, multiculturalism and racism, collectivism and individualism, socialism and capitalism, multiculturalism and colonialism, feminism and patriarchy.

The question of post-poststructuralism (structuralism, or critical structuralism), post-postfeminism (feminism, structural feminism, feminist structuralism), post-post-Marxism (Marxism, structural Marxism, Marxist structuralism), and multiculturalism is not whether texts and realities are structured, but how they are structured in dominance, and how they can be critiqued, rejected, and transformed. The question of post-postmodernism is the question of modernism. In relation to feminism and sexism, Marxism and liberalism, multiculturalism and ethnocentrism, feminism and patriarchy, socialism and capitalism, multiculturalism and colonialism, internationalism and imperialism, the question is an old one: Which side are you on? The question of revolution may not be *the* question at this historical juncture. But the question of resistance is never out of the question.

NOTES

1   Durkheim's Milieu

1. I rely in particular on the chronologies of events in Landes 1988, Boxer and Quataert 1987, and Bell and Offen 1983. Tilly 1981 provides vivid accounts of the participation of women in various political conflicts in nineteenth-century France, along with a detailed analysis of the variation in the status of women and in their motivations for political action according to the political economy of particular regions of France.

2. The condition of women was frequently compared to the condition of slaves by nineteenth-century feminists around the world. In 1794 slavery was abolished in French colonies, while women remained noncitizens in France—much as abolition and Afro-American male suffrage were accomplished prior to female suffrage in the United States. A final irony related to Olympe de Gouges is that she advocated "full equality for all people, even at the cost of the colonies and the French empire" (Landes 1988, 124). For a discussion of the relationship between feminism, slavery, and colonialism, see Ferguson 1992.

3. This is the date of Durkheim's first published work, according to Lukes's bibliography (1985). *The Division of Labor in Society,* Durkheim's major work, appeared in 1893.

4. Very little has been written about Durkheim's "private" or domestic life. It is symptomatic of this aporia that Lukes, Durkheim's definitive biographer, devotes only one page to Durkheim's relationship with his family in general and his wife in particular (1985, 99). Lukes derives this more personal information from Mauss 1968–69 and Davy 1919. According to Mauss, Durkheim's marriage and family exemplified traditional, patriarchal "dual spheres." Davy concurs that Durkheim's family life exactly reflected his "domestic ideal." Ironically, Mauss was writing not about Durkheim but about his wife, Louise, née Dreyfus, and he indicates that in addition to her familial role she collaborated closely with Durkheim on his scholarly work—a fact that directly contradicts Durkheim's description of women's capabilities as well as his prescription for a sexual division of labor. Davy was writing a tribute to Durkheim himself on the occasion of his death. The tribute comprises two parts: "The Man" and "The Work"; however, in the eighteen pages devoted to Durkheim "the man," only one paragraph deals with his family life. The remainder probes Durkheim's emotions and relationships in the "public sphere," vis-à-vis his intellectual and political work and other men. Two additional sources examined Durkheim's personal life. Charle 1984 decries the lack of attention to Durkheim's personal life and the consequent lack of attention to the relationship between his private life and his public life. Charle suggests that Durkheim's social theory can be related to his social position—that is, to his class and race. Specifically, Durkheim's marriage was lucrative for him, and provided him a relatively advantageous class position, which perhaps explains his opposition to class struggle; conversely, his racial status was disadvantageous, which may account for his assimilationism in theory and in practice. Finally, Filloux 1976 provides a sophisticated psychoanalysis of Durkheim's relationship with his father and his son, mediated by the relationship between Judaism and sociology, the rabbinate and the academy. Unfortunately, Filloux illustrates a final irony: just as Durkheim wrote about the history of the family in terms of the shifting relationships between fathers and sons, so his commentators focus on Durkheim's relationship with his son, André, especially on André as Durkheim's pupil and colleague and the way André's death in World War I devastated Durkheim and precipitated his own death.

5. Offen 1987, 183, states that census reports since the mid-nineteenth century "revealed that France had led all other nations with the highest percentage of women active in the labor force. The percentage of the female population

employed in both agricultural and nonagricultural labor rose from 24 percent in 1866 to 38 percent in 1911. Of the several million women in the labor force, the number employed in the nonagricultural sector doubled between 1856 and 1906. . . . The greater proportion of them were young and single, or older and widowed. Still, a sizeable proportion—some 40 percent by 1901—were married women with children." In addition, she notes that by 1911, "over 100,000 women workers belonged to syndicats (unions)." This number was triple the number in 1900, and in addition to the 25,000 women who belonged to all-female unions. Writing in 1896, Jeanne-E. Schmahl reports "4,500,000 work-women, not to speak of authors, musicians, painters, actresses, teachers, shop-assistants, and domestic servants—in all about 6,000,000 women-workers" (Bell and Offen 1983, 2:101).

6. Durkheim's theory of society and his theory of women are heterogeneous and complementary theories, as I hope to demonstrate in this book.

7. I fully recognize that a distinction between the "material" and "ideational" or between the "real" and the "theoretical" aspects of social life is highly problematic, in the light of Althusserian and Foucauldian theory. The distinction I make here is admittedly a heuristic and analytical one.

8. Many historical (and contemporary) accounts elide economic, sexual, cultural, racial, and international issues to focus on political inclusion and exclusion within each nation-state. Boxer and Quataert state it this way: "Pressure for broadening the suffrage and democratic rule was launched most dramatically by those left outside political power and influence in liberal Europe—by women and workers" (1987, 189).

9. The category "neoliberalism" is roughly equivalent to "solidarism," which is more widely used but more narrowly applicable. There is a good discussion of the latter term in Offen 1984, 664–67.

10. Again, the distinction between the discursive and the structural is problematic and to some extent arbitrary. Structures are of course "known" only through discourses, and discourses have their own materiality and reality. Thus the relationship between structures and discourses is complex, perhaps inextricable. The distinction I draw remains heuristic and analytical.

11. I owe immeasurable gratitude to my colleague in the English Department at the University of Nebraska, Moira Ferguson, for guiding me to this invaluable resource.

12. This dichotomy, as well as my classification of various theories and theorists in relation to it, is another problematic and arbitrary distinction. One of the most controversial aspects of this type of categorization is the debate over the relationship between structures and theories of "separate spheres" and femi-

nism. Karen M. Offen (1984, 1986, 1987, 1988) makes a powerful and compelling case for viewing the theory and practice of separate spheres—and reforms grounded in such theory and practice—as legitimate, even particularly viable, forms of feminism, especially in Third Republic France and continental Europe in general. She contrasts this form, "familial" or "relational" feminism, with a more assimilationist, universal individualist form, "individualist" or "integral" feminism, which she associates with Anglo-American feminism. She reports the Continental identification of the sexual division of labor with "the collective interest" and opposition to the sexual division of labor with "individualism." Thus she classifies Durkheim as a "feminist" of sorts (1984, 666–67 and n. 52) in much the same way that Lukes classifies him as "a socialist of sorts" (1985, 546), that is, according to idiosyncratic definitions of feminism and socialism. She also argues forcefully for historically specific, as opposed to ahistorical and abstract, analysis of "feminism" (1988). To some extent I must respectfully disagree with her. I do associate separate spheres with patriarchy rather than with feminism; in fact, I see separate spheres and sexual divisions of labor as integral components of patriarchy. In addition, I maintain that there is a transhistorical relationship between separate spheres and patriarchy, that separate spheres are somehow inherently inimical to feminism. Offen's arguments have convinced me, however, that it is possible, pragmatic, and realistic—even necessary and crucial—to improve women's conditions of existence within extant systems of separate spheres.

13. Durkheim's form of liberalism, it must be stressed, differed significantly from the liberalism of most of his contemporaries: it closely resembles twentieth-century neoliberalism rather than nineteenth-century classic liberalism (see above).

14. The "conditions" of education refer to such issues as whether females should be educated inside or outside the home, by the church or the state, by men or women, segregated from males or integrated with them.

15. I have analyzed all the sources represented in Bell and Offen 1983 that I determined were possibly or probably known to Durkheim. Among these sources I have classified the following as conservatives, or as opposing feminism and supporting patriarchy: Rousseau, de Bonald, de Maistre, Comte, Dupanloup, Keller, Turgeon, Sée, Richer, Roussy, Michelet, Proudhon, *L'Atelier,* Simon and *L'Ouvrière,* Zola, Maine, Bachofen, Darwin, Broca, and Spencer. These categorizations are subject to debate, especially my considering Richer a conservative. I have done so because of his advocacy of separate spheres; Offen would undoubtedly categorize him as a feminist based on his advocacy of

reforms to grant women rights, power, and equality within a system of separate spheres.

16. Again, I demarcate conservatives versus feminists on the issue of separate spheres. Offen would make a further distinction, between advocates of subordination and advocates of egalitarianism *within* a system of dual spheres. I also include as conservatives those who think women's characteristics are different from those of men but equal or even superior—that is, those who think women's unique nature encompasses particular skills such as the ability to manage and economize, special emotional or moral characteristics, and so forth.

17. According to Bell and Offen, several feminists critiqued Rousseau's position prior to Durkheim's era, including Catherine Macaulay-Graham, Mary Wollstonecraft, and Germaine de Staël. Durkheim himself wrote fairly extensively and with approbation on Rousseau. For contemporary commentary on Rousseau, see, e.g., Derrida 1976, Landes 1988, and Pope (in Boxer and Quataert 1987).

18. Unless otherwise indicated, the references in the following sections are all to Bell and Offen 1983.

19. Of course Rousseau does not use the term "feminist," which according to Offen 1988 was not widely used in France until the early 1890s. I am inferring the nature of the positions he is attacking and applying an anachronistic label to them, one that perhaps has historically and culturally specific connotations.

20. This was published in several volumes between 1830 and 1842.

21. This was published in several volumes between 1848 and 1854.

22. Comte says of positivism and its plan for the regeneration and reconstruction of society: "It will find a welcome in those classes only whose good sense has been left unimpaired by our vicious system of education, and whose generous sympathies are allowed to develop themselves freely. It is among women, therefore, and among the working classes that the heartiest supporters of the new doctrine will be found." Further, he says explicitly that "positivism is the only system that can supersede the various subversive schemes that are growing everyday more dangerous to all the relations of domestic and social life. . . . the tendency of the doctrine is to elevate the character of both of these classes [women and workers], and it gives a most energetic sanction to all their legitimate aspirations" (Lenzer 1975, 318–19).

23. "Equality in the position of the two sexes is contrary to their nature, and no tendency to it has at any time been exhibited. All history assures us that with the growth of society the peculiar features of each sex have become not less but more distinct. . . . And thus female life, instead of becoming independent of the

Family is being more and more concentrated in it; while at the same time their proper sphere of moral influence is constantly extending. The two tendencies . . . are inseparably connected. . . . If women were to obtain that equality in the affairs of life which their so-called champions are claiming for them without their wish, not only would they suffer morally, but their social position would be in danger" (Bell and Offen 1983, 1:223–24). These formulations reappear almost verbatim in Durkheim's work, with several key exceptions that will be discussed below. See chapter 4, "The Influence of Positivism upon Women," and chapter 6, "The Religion of Humanity," pp. 372–89 in Lenzer 1975.

24. For Comte's views of marriage, the family, and women as the primary moral and social structures and agents in society, see the two chapters listed above and "The Family," pp. 267–70, in Lenzer 1975.

25. He also proposes to defend "her" against "a certain number of impure women who have been rendered insane by sin"—by which I assume he means "feminists" in contemporary terminology.

26. Allgeier and Allgeier 1991 describe Simon André Tissot as advocating the conservation of all sperm except for direct use in reproduction, a principle that gained wide acceptance among nineteenth-century physicians.

27. See also Gane 1983a and Fenton 1980, 1984.

28. According to Landes 1988, "Women's nature began to be credited as a source of difference *and* as the cause of their superiority, a superiority that was nonetheless reckoned only in the moral and spiritual domain" (170). Concurring with Offen, she reports, "Even those who subscribed to feminist aims often did so on the basis of a culturally gendered doctrine of separate spheres" (172).

29. "Women had been reduced to the status of a legal caste at the same time that the ancien régime legal class system was abolished for men" (Moses 1984, 18).

30. Again, my definition is both arbitrary and anachronistic. Offen would classify my definition of "feminism" as only one type, "individualist" or "integral" feminism, as opposed to "familial" or "relational" feminism (1984, 654). My definition excludes "familial" or "relational" feminism as bound up with a sexual division of labor and dual spheres; however, it is not exclusively an "individualist" orientation (individualism pertaining primarily to liberal forms of feminism) but also embraces structuralist, collectivist, and Marxist forms, and so forth.

31. Among the writers represented in Bell and Offen 1983, both de Gouges and Baudeau were monarchists and liberal or cultural feminists; Maugeret and Knight were Christian feminists; d'Aelders, de Staël, J.-Victoire, de Mauchamps, Schmahl, Pelletier, Crouzet-Benaben, Roussel (also a cultural femi-

nist), Blum, Martin, de Pompéry, d'Héricourt, Lambert (Adam), Condorcet, Naquet, and Ferry were liberal feminists; Daubié, Tristan (a socialist or reformist feminist), Deroin (who could also be classified as a Christian, liberal, cultural, and reformist feminist), Fourier (a socialist, reformist, and utopian communalist feminist), and Auclert (the first self-described "feminist" in France, according to Offen 1988, 126) were socialist feminists; Cabet was a utopian, communalist feminist. I label "reformist feminists" those who took a pro-working class stance as well as a pro-women stance and advocated substantial economic reform for the working class in general and for women in particular. They include Dubuisson, Edwards-Pilliet, Pognon, Mink, and Enfantin. Obviously, precise categorization is difficult; the central issue here is not precise categorization, however, but the demonstrable existence of a wide range of feminist theories and practices, articulated with a wide range of social theories and practices concerning society in general, or men in particular, in Durkheim's structural and discursive milieu.

32. Bell and Offen 1983, 1:71, 439–40, Boxer and Quataert 1987, 115–16, Offen 1987, 180.

33. Bell and Offen 1983, 1:279–80, 365, 510–11. Others pointed to the irony that the Catholic clergy and other opponents of republicanism who allegedly controlled women's political beliefs were themselves allowed to vote.

34. France was one of the last European nations to grant suffrage to women (Boxer and Quataert 1987, 210).

35. A full accomplishment of the right to employment would mean full employment for both sexes at equal wages established in line with the principle of comparable worth.

36. References in the text to Bell and Offen 1983 will be to volume and page number only.

37. Many writers, including some pro-women writers as well as Durkheim, compared women to children. More contemptuous writers compared women to eunuchs or "primitives." Maria Martin pointed out that depriving women of civil rights was tantamount to classifying them "with the insane, with criminals, and with children" (Bell and Offen 1983, 2:231).

38. Fourier was writing in the early 1800s. Charlotte Perkins Gilman enunciated a similar theory, notably in *Women and Economics,* at the end of the century.

39. Mary Wollstonecraft seems particularly important and relevant as the author of one of the first statements of consistent liberalism, that is, one of the first explicit applications of liberal precepts to the woman question. In addition, she wrote in reaction to events and conditions in France. Since Ferry was a

central figure in the drive to secularize intellectual and moral education in France, a drive that was later substantially carried forward by Durkheim, his sociopolitical thought must have been influential as well as parallel to Durkheim's on a number of issues. Lukes adduces that "Durkheim was presumably sympathetic, as was Jaurès, to the republican, positivist Ferry and his aim of creating a national system of secular education" (Lukes 1985, 48). Lukes also places Durkheim, in "his belief in national reintegration through (secular) education . . . within a tradition reaching back, in particular, to the Kantian Renouvier and the Comtian Jules Ferry, who had written that 'the principles of 1789 are the basis of modern French society: the teaching of them must be ensured.' There was, Ferry believed, a need to maintain 'a certain morality of the State, certain doctrines of the State which are important for its conservation'" (Lukes 1985, 355). Ferry not only endorses Mill, however, he advocates equal and integrated education for both sexes. Durkheim, an architect of the French educational system, curiously ignores the burning question of female education and presumably would oppose it. Once again a striking parallel is interrupted by the exceptional question of women. Charlotte Perkins Gilman is relevant not as an influence on Durkheim, but as an example of how the biological analogy, organicism, structural functionalism, and social evolutionism that he favored could produce feminist (and socialist) critical social theory as well as patriarchalist, capitalist, and conservative/reformist social theory. Marianne Weber seems relevant as the sole feminist author Durkheim admits to reading—in his review of and opposition to her work (1978c).

40. Comte was also, by his own account, familiar with the work of Mary Wollstonecraft (Thompson 1976, 202).

41. My contextualization of Durkheim's theory of women is incomplete because I have not addressed the specificity of the linguistic milieu in which he wrote. I have chosen not to deal explicitly with the translation problem for several reasons. First, I believe this problem is germane not only to Durkheim's writing on women, but to all his work. I have commented previously (Lehmann 1993a) on systematic distortions of Durkheim and the ways his meaning gets lost in translation. I did not provide a comprehensive treatment of the problem in my previous comments, however, and I do not even raise the issue here. This is primarily because I feel the issue deserves comprehensive treatment, and I cannot do it justice in the course of attempting to treat another topic comprehensively. I hope others will take up this issue in an extensive study, as I hope others will develop the issue of Durkheim's historical context more fully than I have done here. Second, I have been sensitized, by structuralism as well as by poststructuralism and deconstruction, to the futility of seeking

"the" one real, true, actual, genuine "meaning" of something—the primary text, the original meaning, the ultimate referent in ideational or material reality. Finally, practically, I write for an English-speaking audience that is primarily familiar with Durkheim's work in English, with all its distortions and deviations; thus I analyze the texts that have currency in my own historical and linguistic context.

I will make one comment about translation, and it concerns the title of Durkheim's major work, *De la division du travail social: Etude sur l'organisation des sociétés supérieurs*. This is generally translated as *The Division of Labor in Society*. Besides the telling omission of the subtitle, there is a subtle distinction between *travail social* and "labor in society." The phrase *travail social* would be better translated as "social labor," and social labor more clearly distinguishes the sphere Durkheim intends to address—the specifically social sphere of specifically social labor, that is, men's work—from the sphere he intends to ignore— the asocial sphere of asocial (read biological) labor, that is, women's work. Labor "in society" connotes a more inclusive study: all the labor, including putatively asocial, biological labor, that is performed within and by a society.

2 Descriptions of Women

1. See, for example, March 1982.

2. Even more striking is that his commentators follow suit and discuss Durkheim's sociology of the family without mentioning women. See Bynder 1969 and Simpson 1965.

3. Wityak and Wallace 1981 draw the connection between Durkheim's asocial primitives and his asocial women; Sydie 1987 recognizes that Durkheim views women as more natural and less social than men; Gane 1983b sees Durkheim's women as Other/sacred; Jay 1981 sees them as Other/profane.

4. See Gane's signal work, which explicates the hierarchical implications of differential levels of civilization among various social groups (1983a) and the hierarchical and potentially violent implications of differential levels of civilization between men and women (1983b).

5. Durkheim, of course, invokes the "proof" of cranial size to demonstrate both the difference and the evolutionary exacerbation of that difference, which separates women from men in such a definitive way. See, e.g., Durkheim 1933, 58 and 60. In the latter text Durkheim cites LeBon's findings that "with the progress of civilization the brain of the two sexes differentiates itself more and more," owing to "the considerable development of masculine crania" concomitant with "a stationary or even regressive state of female crania."

6. For Durkheim's theory of uterine descent, see Durkheim 1980, 169–70, 172, 248–49, 264, 265, 267, 272, 274, 280.

7. For Durkheim's theory of the evolution of the family, see Durkheim 1978b, 1965a, 1978c, 1980. Cf. also the family theories of Parsons and Engels.

8. Since mothers also have the attributes of age and blood relations, we must infer that Durkheim is speaking of the father's age and blood relations vis-à-vis the children, not the other potential authority figure, the mother.

9. Of course Durkheim is subtly contradicting himself, since his theory of women suggests that they are devoid of social—mental and moral—characteristics and therefore incapable of social—mental and moral—relationships. Durkheim perhaps felt that marriage is a social relationship for men and a physical relationship for women or that women are partially elevated and consecrated to the social level through marriage, while men are partially debased and desecrated to the physical level.

3 Prescriptions for Women

1. Gane 1983b uncovers an exception to this view. In *Incest,* Durkheim describes primitive sexual relations as radically segregated rather than integrated.

2. Durkheim does not describe "family functions," and the term "affective" implies that they are emotional. It seems likely, however, that by "family functions" he means those natural, physical functions—reproduction, nourishment, cleanliness, etc.—that are universal biological imperatives, in which humans are indistinguishable from animals, and whose performance would require no specifically human, social characteristics.

3. See, e.g., 1980, 256.

4. "Women's sexual needs have less of a mental character because, generally speaking, her mental life is less developed. These needs are more closely related to the needs of the organism, following rather than leading them, and consequently find in them an efficient restraint. Being a more instinctive creature than man, woman has only to follow her instincts to find calmness and peace" (1951, 272).

5. Besnard 1973 deserves credit for calling attention to the article. I should point out that Durkheim does not precisely reverse his findings: he does not retract the actual numbers of his suicide statistics. But he reinterprets these numbers so fundamentally that it effectively constitutes a reversal or retraction. The same numbers that indicate an "effect" in *Suicide* later indicate "no effect," and so on.

6. It must be noted that throughout this article Durkheim uses the term

"individuals" in a very disingenuous way. "Individuals" who would apparently benefit from divorce but whose benefits are more apparent than real, and whose interests are in any case superseded by those of society, can be read as "women." "Individuals" who actually benefit from marriage and who actually suffer from anomie and suicide owing to divorce can be read as "men." If the appropriate terms are substituted for "individuals," the later article reads more like *Suicide.*

7. The issue of whether Durkheim is a conservative, liberal, or radical is one of the most important debates surrounding his work. Coser 1967, Nisbet 1952, 1965, and Zeitlin 1981 have labeled Durkheim a conservative. This view has been contested by Richter 1960. Giddens 1976, Lukes 1985, and Tiryakian 1978 identify Durkheim as a liberal. Pearce 1989 analyzes the radical potential of Durkheim's work. LaCapra 1985 sees Durkheim's work as a synthesis of conservative, radical, and liberal thought. This is also the explicit position of Wallwork 1972 and is implied by Giddens 1971a, 1971b, Lukes 1985, and Szacki 1979. Durkheim can best be classified, overall, as a neoliberal—an advocate of reformed state capitalism and social democracy. Of relevance here is the fact that he takes a liberal (individualist) position with respect to men and a conservative (caste) perspective with respect to women. Even when he endorses a liberal policy—the extension of de jure individual occupational mobility to women—it is with conservative intent: he expects women's natural, differential group "nature" to maintain their caste position in women's work.

4   Contradictions: The Problem of Women

1. On the contradictory relationship between Durkheim's theories of women and his sociological theory, see also Besnard 1973.

2. In general "the wife profits less from family life than the husband. . . . in itself conjugal society is harmful to the woman and aggravates her tendency to suicide" (1951, 188–89).

3. "Man benefits more by it. The liberty he thus renounces could only be a source of torment to him. Woman did not have the same reasons to abandon it . . . by submitting to the same rule, it was she who made the sacrifice" (1951, 276).

4. "She thus does not require so strict a social regulation as marriage, and particularly as monogamic marriage. . . . By limiting the horizon, it closes all egress and forbids even legitimate hope. . . . marriage is not in the same degree useful to her for limiting her desires, which are naturally limited, and for teaching her to be contented with her lot; but it prevents her from changing it if it becomes intolerable" (1951, 272).

5. "Consequently, everything that makes it more flexible and lighter can only better the wife's situation. So divorce protects her and she has frequent recourse to it" (1951, 272).

6. "To be sure, we have no reason to suppose that women may ever be able to fulfill the same functions in society as man; but she will be able to play a part in society which, while peculiarly her own, may yet be more active and important than that of today. . . . Both sexes would approximate each other by their very differences. They would be socially equalized, but in different ways" (1951, 385).

7. "These differences will become of greater social use than in the past. Why . . . should not aesthetic functions become woman's as man, more and more absorbed by functions of utility, has to renounce them?" (1951, 385).

8. For example, "Marriage is capable of exercising a moral influence, especially on the male sex." Or again, "Man can be happy and can satisfy his desires in a normal way only if he is regulated, contained, moderated and disciplined." Marriage "gives the man a moral posture which increases his forces of resistance" (1978a, 247).

9. "In order to have separate personalities . . . an individualizing factor is necessary. It is the body that fulfills this function." However, "individuation is not the essential characteristic of the personality." In fact, "the senses, the body and . . . all that individualizes" constitute "the antagonist of the personality." "So it is not at all true that we are more personal as we are more individualized. The two terms are in no way synonymous: in one sense, they oppose more than they imply one another. . . . those who insist upon all the social elements of the individual do not mean by that to deny or debase the personality. They merely refuse to confuse it with the fact of individuation" (1965b, 305–8).

10. The parallels between Durkheim's "dualism of human nature" and Judeo-Christian theology, Freudian theory, and symbolic interactionism are striking.

11. Again, Gane 1983b sees Durkheim's women as Other/sacred; Jay 1981 sees them as Other/profane.

12. For Durkheim, liberty is the "fruit" or the "product" of regulation. "The individual submits to society and this submission is the condition of his liberation" (1953, 72–73).

13. "That which makes us human beings is the amount that we manage to assimilate of ideas, beliefs and precepts for conduct that we call civilization. . . . deprive man of all that society has given him and he is reduced to his sensations. He becomes a being more or less indistinct from an animal" (1953, 56).

14. On Durkheim's views of women and "primitives," see Wityak and Wallace 1981 and Fenton 1980, 1984.

15. The "cult of the individual" is equally the "cult of personality," the "religion of humanity," and the "cult of man."

16. Again, Durkheim has been labeled a conservative, a liberal, and a radical. His work has also been interpreted as a synthesis of conservative, liberal, and radical thought. See below for a related position: Durkheim combines elements of conservatism, liberalism, and radicalism into a sort of neoliberalism—essentially a reformist, statist "social" liberalism.

17. Actually, Durkheim hedges here. He insists that modern productive skills are learned rather than innate, to explain the necessary and imminent disappearance of hereditary occupational distribution. On the other hand, he consistently describes individual mobility as a system that aligns individuals with occupations according to their innate abilities. So he seems to deny the inheritance of skills at the group level but to affirm it at the individual level. See below, chapter 5.

18. The Durkheimian origins of the Davis and Moore stratification scheme are obvious.

19. Again, Durkheim characterizes women's structural capacity and functional activity as "affective." This term certainly connotes emotional structures and functions. Durkheim never explicitly discusses the term "affective," however, and it seems more likely that he views family functions in terms of the biological functions (reproduction, nutrition, cleanliness, etc.) that humans share with all animal species and that asocial women are capable of performing.

20. Pateman 1988, for example, articulates the interrelated spheres theory with respect to liberalism and capitalism in general.

21. Besnard 1973, Johnson 1972, and Tiryakian 1978, for example, tend to present Durkheim's views on women as "prejudices," as the intrusion of ambient ideology into his scientific theory. With characteristic acuity, Pope 1976 acknowledges that Durkheim's theory of women contradicts his theory of suicide and that he deploys biological determinism to explain the difference between men and women as well as the nature of women. However, Pope believes that Durkheim's treatment of sexually differentiated rates of suicide is problematic because of his dogmatic insistence on social determinism and his concomitant refusal to explicitly and systematically recognize biological factors (e.g., sex and age) as causal variables.

22. Besnard 1973 and Gane 1983b, for example, allude to the exclusion of women from the apparently universal categories *l'homme, l'humanité,* or "humans." Gane also holds the opinion that Durkheim's views on women are systematic, coherent, and deliberate theoretical structures rather than ideological contingencies.

5 Theories of Race, Class, and Sex

1. See 1951, 85.

2. "As we advance, the human varieties which are formed become, then, less hereditary. These varieties are less and less racial" (1933, 309).

3. The "hereditary likenesses" that constitute race are quintessentially "physical characteristics." But these "organic properties" are ultimately "neither numerous enough nor distinctive enough" to classify "anthropological types" (1933, 309). Eventually "morphological differences are obliterated." In modern society "morphological types are levelling off" (1933, 335).

4. See 1933, 305, 318.

5. See 1933, 306.

6. See 1933, 318.

7. "The hereditary contribution diminishes, not only in relative value, but in absolute value. Heredity becomes a lesser factor of human development, not only because there is an ever greater multitude of new acquisitions it cannot transmit, but also because those it transmits disturb individual variations less" (1933, 321).

8. See 1933, 323.

9. See 1933, 327. It is crucial to note that Durkheim's characteristic ambiguity leaves room for hereditary castes in modern societies. The genetic transmission of *general* aptitudes to distinct *classes* could coincide with the social transmission of *specific* aptitudes to distinct individuals *within* each class.

10. More specifically, since society is itself natural, the pinnacle of nature, this evolution represents the gradual transcendence of the complex and psychic dimension of nature over the simple and physical.

11. See 1933, xxi, 333, 336.

12. See 1933, 345–46. Durkheim is ambiguous with respect to aptitude in a second sense. He suggests that ability is natural (innate at the individual level) and that it is social (learned). See also Fenton 1984, 58.

13. See 1951, bk. 1, chap. 2, passim.

14. Lukes 1985, e.g., 332–49, 41, 557.

15. See 1899, 59–62.

16. Quoted in Lukes 1985.

17. Ibid.

18. Ibid.

19. Ibid.

20. Ibid.

21. The only comprehensive treatment of Durkheim's theory of race is by Fenton (1980, 1984), who points out that Durkheim is consistent with his own sociologism with respect to race, and that his opposition to biological/racial reductionism constitutes an original theoretical opposition to racism. Durkheim's advocacy of achievement over ascription, cultural over biological determinism, and social over racial explanation *is* prescient and progressive. However, his dismissal of "race" as a social category, racism as a social belief, and racialism as a social practice is premature and problematic. Additionally, he stumbles into a fundamental liberal quagmire when he speaks of ability as innate, that is, genetically inherited, *and* specific to each individual—unrelated to the aptitudes of the individual's biological group. Fenton provides a brilliant and definitive analysis of the ambiguous implications of Durkheim's theory with respect to colonial attitudes and relations.

22. "The social question . . . no longer opposes the source of technic to that of power, as two antagonists . . . it no longer stirs questions of classes; it no longer opposes rich to poor, employers to workers . . . the social question, posed this way, is not a question of money or force; it is a question of moral agents. What dominates it is not the state of our economy but the state of our morality" (1958, 204). The social problem is not the problem of capitalism, but of anarchy in the economy: "This state of anarchy comes about not from this machinery being in these hands and not in those, but because the activity deriving from it is not regulated" (1957, 31).

23. See, e.g., 1958, 203; 1951, 378–84, 389–91.

24. See 1933, 376–77.

25. "Equality in the external conditions of conflict is not only necessary to attach each individual to his function, but also to link functions to one another" (1933, 381).

26. Cf. Marx, for whom "fair" wages are impossible.

27. Socialism is both incorrect and impossible because it seeks to satisfy rather than to limit economic aspirations. "For it is in vain that one will create privileges for workers which neutralize in part those enjoyed by employers; in vain will the working day be decreased or even wages legally increased. We will not succeed in pacifying roused appetites, because they will acquire new force in the measure they are appeased. There are no limits possible to their requirements. To undertake to appease them by satisfying them is to hope to fill the vessel of the Danaides" (1958, 57).

28. The only exceptions, of course, are transitional phenomena, which are simultaneously negative and general, but also necessary and temporary.

29. "The normality of a phenomenon is to be explained by the mere fact that it is bound up with the conditions of existence of the species under consideration, either as a mechanically necessary effect of these conditions or as a means permitting the organisms to adapt themselves" (1938, 60).

30. See 1958.

31. Durkheim wants to mediate the separation, in theory and reality, between the state and civil society. He opposes the dichotomy between "social functions" of general social interest, concerning "the social body in its entirety," which are represented by the state, and "individual" or "economic" functions and private economic interests: "All the functions of a society are social" (1958, 18). "According to socialism . . . economic functions . . . must be socially organized" (1958, 35).

32. Socialism calls for "linking," "organizing and centralizing," and "regulating" economic activity (1958, 19, 47, 52).

33. "Socialism . . . is above all an aspiration for a rearrangement of the social structure, by relocating the industrial set-up in the totality of the social organism, drawing it out of the shadow where it was functioning automatically, summoning it to the light and to the control of the conscience" (1958, 26).

34. For other commentaries on Durkheim's treatment of economics, class, social hierarchy, occupational groups, capitalism, and socialism, see, e.g.: Benoit-Smullyan 1948; Bottomore 1981; Coser 1967; Fenton 1980, 1984; Gane 1983a, 1984, 1988; Giddens 1971a, 1971b, 1976; Horowitz 1979; LaCapra 1985; Lukes 1985; Meštrović 1988; Morris 1978; Nisbet 1952, 1965; Pearce 1989; Poggi 1973; Tiryakian 1978; Wallwork 1972; and Zeitlin 1981.

35. More precisely, women represent the extrasocial condition of possibility of the social subject, the biological factor that provides the material substratum of the social organism by physically reproducing individual male bodies.

36. The "place in society," "respect," "grandeur," "status," "authority," "juridical condition," "moral importance," "moral equality," etc., of women depend on the "organic unity" and "religious respect" of the family. See, e.g., 1978c, 140, 144; 1980, 209, 274–75, 303.

37. See 1933, 56–61; 1980, 209, 218, 256, 260, 292, 303; 1978c, 143; 1951, 259–76; 1978a.

38. Obviously, Durkheim eliminates the category of class as caste, or distribution mechanism, once the natural foundation of the social institution of caste—race—is eliminated. Like all liberals and structural functionalists, however, he does not, as seen above, eliminate the category of class as *outcome,* as the hierarchical arrangement of individuals based on their unequal natural abilities and unequal social values.

6   The Contemporary Milieu

1. Of course the distinction between "political" and "apodictic" discourse is arbitrary and problematic. I intend it to signify the difference between explicitly political and practical rhetoric, which directly prescribes certain forms of social organization, and allegedly apodictic and speculative rhetoric, which putatively "merely" describes reality. Actually, I find scientific "description" very political and prescriptive and programmatic "prescription" very scientific and descriptive. Both are forms of "theory."

2. I am grateful to Rosalind Sydie for reminding me to mention the significance of Freudian and Lacanian psychoanalysis, as well as Saussurian linguistic theory in the constitution of "new French feminism," which, in its superabundant complexity, "contains" structuralist, critical structuralist, and poststructuralist tendencies, essentialist, radical empiricist, and social determinist tendencies, and so on. See, e.g., Marks and de Courtivron 1981 and Moi 1987.

3. See Besnard 1973.

4. I refer primarily, but not exclusively, to the early work of Foucault, the early work of Derrida, the late work of Barthes, one tendency within Lacan, the work of Kristeva, and so on—that is, the Francophone pantheon of poststructuralists.

5. Neostructural functionalists focus on the way liberalism has supplanted all other ideologies to become identified as universal truth ("the end of ideology"; Bell 1960), the way capitalism has supplanted all other social structures to become identified as universal reality ("the end of history"; Fukuyama 1992), and the way capitalism is evolving into an ultimately adaptive utopia ("postindustrial society"; Bell 1969). Structural functionalism has claimed its nontheoretical (uncontested) status as "truth" before. See Davis 1959.

6. See, e.g., Callinicos 1990 and Modleski 1991.

7. However, I can only surmise that the rush to poststructuralism on the part of critical theory is seen as a victory for "the powers (and knowledges) that be."

8. I am speaking primarily of anarchism and humanist Marxism, but classic individualistic, laissez-faire liberalism demonstrates similar tendencies.

9. The epitome of this type of theorizing must be the fatalistic liberal, individualistic humanism of Marcuse's *One-Dimensional Man*. Similarly, poststructuralists conceptualize human beings as totally determinate (spoken by language, thought by discourse, etc.) and totally indeterminate (different and deferred, perhaps believing in science and social structures, but not *necessarily* determined by them).

10. This is the Nietzschean, Lukácsian, poststructuralist, postmodernist, deconstructionist tendency.

11. See Lehmann 1993a, 1993b.

12. I am most familiar with this problem in the treatment, neglect, caricaturizing, and vilification of Marxism in feminist theory and research.

13. Cultural studies, like feminism, Marxism, and multiculturalism, is charting the terrain occupied by, alternatively, structuralist tendencies and poststructuralist tendencies. My objective is not so much to proselytize on behalf of critical structuralism as to delineate it in a meaningful, if crude, way from structural functionalism and from poststructuralism. This is why I focus so much on definition, which, like Karen Offen (1988), I do not eschew but embrace. For a discussion of cultural studies as critical theory, see Agger 1992. For a contrasting view of cultural studies, as a Durkheimian legacy and enterprise, see Alexander 1988.

14. See Jaggar and Rothenberg's *Feminist Frameworks,* 3d ed. (1993) for an introduction to these terms and classifications (or integrations).

15. See Monique Wittig, "One Is Not Born a Woman," in Jaggar and Rothenberg 1993. She advocates destroying "men" and "women," which destruction would create "the necessity of existing as a person" (182).

16. The model of "vertical" and "horizontal" struggle is drawn from Audre Lorde's essay "Scratching the Surface," in Jaggar and Rothenberg 1984.

REFERENCES

Agger, Ben. 1992. *Cultural Studies as Critical Theory.* London: Falmer Press.

Alexander, Jeffrey C., ed. 1988. *Durkheimian Sociology: Cultural Studies.* Cambridge: Cambridge University Press.

Allgeier, Albert, and Elizabeth Allgeier. 1991. *Sexual Interactions.* Lexington, Mass.: D. C. Heath.

Bell, Daniel. 1960. *The End of Ideology: On the Exhaustion of Political Ideas in the Fifties.* Glencoe, Ill.: Free Press.

———. 1969. *The Coming of Post-industrial Society.* New York: Basic Books.

Bell, Susan Groag, and Karen M. Offen, eds. 1983. *Women, the Family, and Freedom: The Debate in Documents,* Vols. 1 and 2. Stanford: Stanford University Press.

Benoit-Smullyan, Emile. 1948. "The Sociologism of Emile Durkheim and His School." In *An Introduction to the History of Sociology,* edited by Harry Barnes, 499–537. Chicago: University of Chicago Press.

Benton, Ted. 1977. *Philosophical Foundations of the Three Sociologies.* London: Routledge and Kegan Paul.

Besnard, Philippe. 1973. "Durkheim et les femmes, ou Le *Suicide* inachevé." *Revue Française de Sociologie* 14:27–61.

Bologh, Roslyn W. 1990. *Love or Greatness: Max Weber and Masculine Thinking—a Feminist Inquiry.* Boston: Unwin Hyman.

Bottomore, Tom. 1981. "A Marxist Consideration of Durkheim." *Social Forces* 59, no. 4:902–17.

Boxer, Marilyn J., and Jean H. Quataert, eds. 1978. *Socialist Women: European Socialist Feminism in the Nineteenth and Early Twentieth Centuries.* New York: Elsevier.

——. 1987. *Connecting Spheres: Women in the Western World, 1500 to the Present.* New York: Oxford University Press.

Brantlinger, Patrick. 1990. *Crusoe's Footprints: Cultural Studies in Britain and America.* New York: Routledge.

Bynder, Herbert. 1969. "Emile Durkheim and the Sociology of the Family." *Journal of Marriage and the Family* 31:527–33.

Callinicos, Alex. 1990. *Against Postmodernism: A Marxist Critique.* New York: St. Martin's Press.

Cashion, Barbara G. 1970. "Durkheim's Concept of Anomie and Its Relationship to Divorce." *Sociology and Social Research* 55:72–81.

Charle, Christophe. 1984. "Le beau mariage d'Emile Durkheim." *Actes de la Recherche en Sciences Sociales* 55:45–49.

Coser, Lewis A. 1967. "Durkheim's Conservatism and Its Implications for Sociological Theory." In *Continuities in the Study of Social Conflict.* New York: Free Press.

Davis, Kingsley. 1959. "The Myth of Functional Analysis as a Special Method in Sociology and Anthropology." *American Sociological Review* 24, no. 6:757–72.

Davy, Georges. 1919. "Emile Durkheim: I, L'homme." *Revue de Métaphysique et de Morale* 26:181–98.

Derrida, Jacques. 1976. *Of Grammatology.* Baltimore: Johns Hopkins University Press.

Durkheim, Emile. 1888. "Cours de science sociale: Leçon d'ouverture." *Revue Internationale de l'Enseignement* 15:23–48.

——. 1899. Contribution. In *Enquête sur l'antisémitisme,* edited by Henri Dagan, 59–63. Paris: P. V. Stock.

——. 1933. *The Division of Labor in Society.* 1893. New York: Free Press.

——. 1938. *The Rules of Sociological Method.* 1895. Glencoe, Ill.: Free Press.

——. 1951. *Suicide.* 1897. New York: Free Press.

——. 1953. *Sociology and Philosophy.* 1924. Glencoe, Ill.: Free Press.

——. 1957. *Professional Ethics and Civic Morals.* 1950. London: Routledge and Kegan Paul.

——. 1958. *Socialism and Saint-Simon.* 1928. Yellow Springs, Ohio: Antioch Press.

——. 1960. "The Dualism of Human Nature and Its Social Conditions." 1914. In *Emile Durkheim,* edited by Kurt Wolff, 325–40. Columbus: Ohio State University Press.

——. 1961. *Moral Education.* 1925. New York: Free Press.

——. 1963a. *Incest: The Nature and Origin of the Taboo.* 1898. New York: Lyle Stuart.

——. 1963b. *Primitive Classification.* 1903. Chicago: University of Chicago Press.

——. 1965a. "The Conjugal Family." 1892. In "A Durkheim Fragment," by George Simpson, *American Journal of Sociology* 70:528–36.

——. 1965b. *The Elementary Forms of the Religious Life.* 1912. New York: Free Press.

——. 1969. "Individualism and the Intellectuals." 1898. *Political Studies* 27, no. 1:14–30.

——. 1978a. "Divorce by Mutual Consent." 1906. In *Emile Durkheim on Institutional Analysis,* edited by Mark Traugott, 240–52. Chicago: University of Chicago Press.

——. 1978b. "Introduction to the Sociology of the Family." 1888. In *Emile Durkheim on Institutional Analysis,* edited by Mark Traugott, 205–28. Chicago: University of Chicago Press.

——. 1978c. "Review of Marianne Weber, *Ehefrau und Mutter in der Rechtsentwickelung.*" 1910. In *Emile Durkheim on Institutional Analysis,* edited by Mark Traugott, 139–44. Chicago: University of Chicago Press.

——. 1979. *Essays on Morals and Education,* edited by W.S.F. Pickering. London: Routledge and Kegan Paul.

——. 1980. *Contributions to L'Année Sociologique,* edited by Yash Nandan. New York: Free Press.

Faludi, Susan. 1991. *Backlash: The Undeclared War against American Women.* New York: Crown.

Fenton, C. Stephen. 1980. "Race, Class and Politics in the Work of Emile Durkheim." In *Sociological Theories: Race and Colonialism,* edited by UNESCO, Paris: UNESCO, 143–82.

——. 1984. "Race and Society: Primitive and Modern." In *Durkheim and Modern Sociology,* by Steve Fenton, 116–42. Cambridge: Cambridge University Press.

Ferguson, Moira. 1992. *Subject to Others: British Women Writers and Colonial Slavery, 1670–1834.* New York: Routledge.

Filloux, Jean-Claude. 1976. "Il ne faut pas oublier que je suis fils de rabbin." *Revue Française de Sociologie* 17, no. 2:259–66.

Fox-Genovese, Elizabeth. 1991. *Feminism without Illusions: A Critique of Individualism.* Chapel Hill: University of North Carolina Press.

Fukuyama, Francis. 1992. *The End of History and the Last Man.* New York: Free Press.

Gane, Mike. 1983a. "Durkheim: The Sacred Language." *Economy and Society* 12:1–47.

———. 1983b. "Durkheim: Woman as Outsider." *Economy and Society* 12:227–70.

———. 1984. "Institutional Socialism and the Sociological Critique of Communism." *Economy and Society* 13:305–30.

———. 1988. *On Durkheim's Rules of Sociological Method.* London: Routledge.

Giddens, Anthony. 1971a. *Capitalism and Modern Social Theory.* Cambridge: Cambridge University Press.

———. 1971b. "Durkheim's Political Sociology." *Sociological Review* 19:477–519.

———. 1976. "Classical Social Theory and the Origins of Modern Sociology." *American Journal of Sociology* 81:703–29.

Hirst, P. Q. 1973. "Morphology and Pathology: Biological Analogies and Metaphors in Durkheim's *The Rules of Sociological Method.*" *Economy and Society* 2:1–34.

———. 1975. *Durkheim, Bernard and Epistemology.* London: Routledge.

Horowitz, Irving Louis. 1979. "On the Expansion of New Theories and the Withering Away of Old Classes." *Society* 16, no. 2 (118):55–62.

Jaggar, Alison, and Paula Rothenberg. 1984. *Feminist Frameworks: Alternative Theoretical Accounts of the Relations between Women and Men.* 2d ed. New York: McGraw-Hill.

———. 1993. *Feminist Frameworks: Alternative Theoretical Accounts of the Relations between Women and Men.* 3d ed. New York: McGraw-Hill.

Jay, Nancy. 1981. "Gender and Dichotomy." *Feminist Studies* 7:38–56.

Johnson, Barclay. 1972. "Durkheim on Women." In *Woman in a Man-Made World,* edited by Nona Glazer-Malbin and Helen Youngelson Waehrer, 164–67. Chicago: Rand-McNally.

Johnson, Kathryn K. 1979. "Durkheim Revisited: 'Why Do Women Kill Themselves?'" *Suicide and Life-Threatening Behavior* 9:145–53.

Johnson, Richard. 1986/87. "What Is Cultural Studies Anyway?" *Social Text* 16:38–80.

Jordanova, L. J. 1980. "Natural Facts: A Historical Perspective on Science and Sexuality." In *Nature, Culture and Gender,* edited by Carol P. MacCormack and Marilyn Strathern, 42–69. New York: Cambridge University Press.

Kandal, Terry R. 1988. *The Woman Question in Classical Sociological Theory.* Miami: Florida International University Press.

Keat, Russell, and John Urry. 1975. *Social Theory as Science.* London: Routledge and Kegan Paul.

LaCapra, Dominick. 1985. *Emile Durkheim: Sociologist and Philosopher.* Chicago: University of Chicago Press.

Landes, Joan B. 1988. *Women and the Public Sphere in the Age of the French Revolution.* Ithaca: Cornell University Press.

Lehmann, Jennifer M. 1990. "Durkheim's Response to Feminism: Prescriptions for Women." *Sociological Theory* 8, no. 2:163–87.

———. 1991. "Durkheim's Women: His Theory of the Structures and Functions of Sexuality." *Current Perspectives in Social Theory* 11:141–67.

———. 1993a. *Deconstructing Durkheim: A Post-post-structuralist Critique.* New York: Routledge.

———. 1993b. "The Undecidability of Derrida/The Premature Demise of Althusser." *Current Perspectives in Social Theory* 13:109–38.

Lenzer, Gertrud, ed. 1975. *Auguste Comte and Positivism: The Essential Writings.* New York: Harper Torchbooks.

Lukes, Steven. 1985. *Emile Durkheim: His Life and Work.* Stanford: Stanford University Press.

March, Artemis. 1982. "Female Invisibility in Androcentric Sociological Theory." *Insurgent Sociologist* 11, no. 2:99–107.

Marks, Elaine, and Isabelle de Courtivron, eds. 1981. *New French Feminisms: An Anthology.* New York: Schocken Books.

Mauss, Marcel. 1968–69. "Notices biographiques." 1927. In *Oeuvres,* edited by Victor Karady, 523–24. Paris: Editions de Minuit.

Mayes, Sharon S. 1980. "Sociological Thought in Emile Durkheim and George Fitzhugh." *British Journal of Sociology* 31:78–94.

Mestrovic, Stjepan. 1988. *Emile Durkheim and the Reformation of Sociology.* Totowa, N.J.: Rowman and Littlefield.

Modleski, Tania. 1991. *Feminism without Women: Culture and Criticism in a "Postfeminist" Age.* New York: Routledge.

Moi, Toril, ed. 1987. *French Feminist Thought: A Reader.* Oxford: Basil Blackwell.

Moon, S. Joan. 1978. "Feminism and Socialism: The Utopian Synthesis of Flora Tristan." In *Socialist Women: European Socialist Feminism in the Nineteenth and Early Twentieth Centuries,* edited by Marilyn J. Boxer and Jean H. Quataert, 19–50. New York: Elsevier.

Morris, Brian. 1978. "Are There Any Individuals in India? A Critique of Dumont's Theory of the Individual." *Eastern Anthropologist* 31, no. 4:365–77.

Moses, Claire Goldberg. 1984. *French Feminism in the Nineteenth Century.* Albany: State University of New York Press.

Nisbet, Robert A. 1952. "Conservatism and Sociology." *American Journal of Sociology* 58:167–75.

——. 1965. *Emile Durkheim.* Englewood Cliffs, N.J.: Prentice-Hall.

Nizan, Paul. 1971. *The Watchdogs: Philosophers of the Established Order.* New York: Monthly Review Press.

Offen, Karen M. 1984. "Depopulation, Nationalism, and Feminism in Fin-de-Siècle France." *American Historical Review* 89, no. 3:648–76.

——. 1986. "Ernest Legouvé and the Doctrine of 'Equality in Difference' for Women: A Case Study of Male Feminism in Nineteenth-Century French Thought." *Journal of Modern History* 58:452–84.

——. 1987. "Feminism, Antifeminism, and National Family Politics in Early Third Republic France." In *Connecting Spheres: Women in the Western World, 1500 to the Present,* edited by Marilyn J. Boxer and Jean H. Quataert, 177–86. New York: Oxford University Press.

——. 1988. "Defining Feminism: A Comparative Historical Approach." *Signs: Journal of Women in Culture and Society* 14, no. 1:119–57.

Ollenburger, Jane C., and Helen A. Moore. 1992. *A Sociology of Women: The Intersection of Patriarchy, Capitalism and Colonization.* Englewood Cliffs, N.J.: Prentice-Hall.

Pateman, Carole. 1988. *The Sexual Contract.* Stanford: Stanford University Press.

Pearce, Frank. 1989. *The Radical Durkheim.* Boston: Unwin Hyman.

Poggi, Gianfranco. 1973. *Images of Society: Essays on the Sociological Theories of Tocqueville, Marx, and Durkheim.* Stanford: Stanford University Press.

Pope, Barbara Corrado. 1987. "The Influence of Rousseau's Ideology of Domesticity." In *Connecting Spheres: Women in the Western World, 1500 to the Present,* edited by Marilyn J. Boxer and Jean H. Quataert, 136–45. New York: Oxford University Press.

Pope, Whitney. 1976. *Durkheim's "Suicide": A Classic Analyzed.* Chicago: University of Chicago Press.

Richter, Melvin. 1960. "Durkheim's Politics and Political Theory." In *Emile Durkheim: Essays on Sociology and Philosophy,* edited by Kurt Wolff, 170–210. Columbus: Ohio State University Press.

Roth, Guenther. 1990. "Durkheim and the Principles of 1789." *Telos* 82:71–88.

Sharma, Arvind. 1978. "Emile Durkheim on Suttee as Suicide." *International Journal of Contemporary Sociology* 15:283–91.

Simpson, George. 1965. "A Durkheim Fragment." *American Journal of Sociology* 70:527–36.

Swierenga, Robert P. 1977. "Ethnicity in Historical Perspective." *Social Science* 52, no. 1:31–44.

Sydie, R. A. 1987. *Natural Women, Cultured Men: A Feminist Perspective on Sociological Theory.* New York: New York University Press.

Szacki, Jerzy. 1979. *History of Sociological Thought.* Westport, Conn.: Greenwood Press.

Therborn, Goran. 1976. *Science, Class and Society.* London: New Left Books.

Thompson, Kenneth, ed. 1976. *August Comte: The Foundation of Sociology.* New York: John Wiley.

Tilly, Louise A. 1981. "Women's Collective Action and Feminism in France, 1870–1914." In *Class Conflict and Collective Action,* edited by Louise A. Tilly and Charles Tilly, 207–31. Beverly Hills, Calif.: Sage.

Tiryakian, Edward A. 1978. "Emile Durkheim." In *A History of Sociological Analysis,* by Tom Bottomore and Robert Nisbet, 187–236. New York: Basic Books.

——. 1981. "Sexual Anomie, Social Structure, Societal Change." *Social Forces* 59:1025–53.

Traugott, Mark, ed. 1978. *Emile Durkheim on Institutional Analysis.* Chicago: University of Chicago Press.

Van den Berghe, Pierre L. 1975. "Integration and Conflict in Multinational States." *Social Dynamics* 1, no. 1:3–10.

Wallwork, Ernest. 1972. *Durkheim, Morality and Milieu.* Cambridge: Cambridge University Press.

Wityak, Nancy L., and Ruth A. Wallace. 1981. "Durkheim's Non-social Facts about Primitives and Women." *Sociological Inquiry* 51:61–67.

Zeitlin, Irving. 1981. *Ideology and the Development of Sociological Theory.* Englewood Cliffs, N.J.: Prentice-Hall.

INDEX